CRAZY CHRONICLES
OF A PARISH LIFE

Michael Collins

CRAZY
CHRONICLES
of a
PARISH LIFE

columba press

First published in 2017 by
columbᴀ press
23 Merrion Square,
Dublin 2, Co. Dublin
www.columbapress.ie

Cover by Alba Esteban
Origination by Columba Press
Illustrations by Joe Connolly
Printed by Jellyfish Solutions

ISBN 978 1 78218 317 4

Contents

Articles

Scripts

Foreword

Michael Collins claims that I am responsible for his writing career, that it was I who initially encouraged him to put pen to paper. That is akin to saying that someone was responsible for sending Scott off to explore the Antarctic.

The truth is that Michael Collins was a born chronicler. It was in his DNA. It found its initial expression with photography and film but it was always going to end up with the written word.

If I did encourage him to write, it was because he was a good preacher. That is detectable in the faces and the posture of a congregation on a Sunday morning. There is a quiet but detectable response from a congregation when the sacristy door opens and a good preacher enters the sanctuary.

Collins had a voice that attracted an audience and he had the words that held their attention and their interest. Most importantly, he knew that spirituality and theology had their essence in the 'bits and pieces of everyday life'. The Scriptures are, after all, a bundle of the stories of men and women living on the earth from earlier times trying to find purpose and meaning.

It would be easy to chronicle the eccentricities and the foibles of people with an analytical and objective correctness, most especially clerics, and while Collins' observations always seem accurate and telling, they are never cruel. He observes with compassion and humour and from within the circle of fragile humanity.

The reader will be able to open this book frequently and it will answer the different moods that life throws out. Sometimes it will be for the humour, the stories of priests and parishioners that are stranger than fiction, other times for the mellowness that the stories of life and death evokes. The history of the author himself is worth a read and then a reread. Colourful and exotic within the rural and urban settings of the north-west of Ireland, and confirming again that all politics, all good drama and all good stories are local.

This is one of those books I will keep beside my bed and I will dip into it fairly often. I know right well that there will be plenty of others who will be doing the same. There will be some who will find themselves reading into the small hours of the morning.

Denis Bradley

Fading Fast

⁓✲⁓

Let me begin, not just at the beginning, but before the beginning.

On the cover of a book about a prison ship called the *Argenta*, in which anti-partitionist troublemakers were interned without trial in the early 1920s, there is a photograph of eleven early residents, and second from the right in the front row, with a smile on his face and a cigarette in his hand, is my father.

I don't think he really qualified as a terrorist. He never did anything significantly wrong, but like many of his fellow countrymen, he just did not like the idea of a border, especially since it would be running past his doorstep; he probably kept the wrong company, and said the wrong things and, as a consequence, finished up on the prison ship.

We often asked him about life on board but he never parted with any information. We asked him what terrible things he had done which caused him to be interned, but the worst that he could recount was that he and some others had cut down a tree across the road to block the British army transports. This lack of heroic enterprise was due no doubt to the fact, which he admitted later, that there was only one gun – and a shotgun at that – between the whole platoon.

When he was an old man, my brother asked him to write his life story, hoping that he might tell us something about life on the prison ship, and he duly wrote all nine pages of it. And where did he begin? Not with the day he set foot on the *Argenta*, but with the day he left it. I suppose we should not have expected anything else. After all, he did not even give his marriage a full sentence: 'In the meantime, I had got married...', he tells us. And that gives you an idea how much communication there was between my father and his family.

My mother was a more down-to-earth person and dealt with the realities of life. They got married in the late 1920s and went to live in Glasgow because that was where my father could best carry out his calling as a cattle dealer. My elder brother and sister were born there, but the family moved back after a few years to home territory in Castlederg where I was born. When I was a month old, we moved to a farm near Omagh where the family lived for the next sixty years.

My childhood was entirely taken up with life on the farm, where work was the order of the day. Even though we lived in a thirteen-room farmhouse and had hot and cold running water, a bathroom, an indoor toilet, a telephone and an Aga cooker – and that was not bad for the 1930s – we still regarded ourselves as poor. Others might boast to their neighbours of their new high-powered modern Aga cooker, but one of my most vivid memories is of a large sow and a litter of piglets firmly established for warmth at the side of the Aga. Everything had a practical use and appearances did not count for anything.

We had fifty acres of land and kept nine or ten milking cows, along with the usual hens and pigs. Essentially, the day began at seven o'clock with my father coming into the bedroom, taking the bedclothes in his hand and sweeping them onto the floor with the command, 'Up'. It was easier to get up and get dressed rather than lie in the cold without any covering. From there we all went to do our chores, and one of mine was to help with milking the cows.

Let me give you some guidance on the milking of cows by hand, should you ever be called upon to perform such a task. It was not the cosy Technicolor procedure exemplified by romantic pictures of Swiss milkmaids with their white aprons and wooden pails! It was a messy, hazardous operation where you had to pit your wits against a bunch of bored and thick-witted cows with nothing on their mind other than making life as difficult as possible for you.

Your first task was to divide the long hairs at the end of the cow's tail around the cow's leg before tying them in a firm knot.

There is nothing more painful or disgusting than a slap across the face with a soggy, smelly and shitty cow's tail, especially if your mouth is open at the moment of impact. Take it from me, there was nothing romantic about milking cows by hand in the 1930s.

The milk was strained through a gauze-type filter into a large metal creamery can and then immersed in a tank of cold water. The cans were usually conveyed by my father in the back seat of his Morris Eight to Nestlé's factory, a mile or so down the road. However, if he were indisposed for any reason, I was called upon to transport the milk in a cart pulled by a laid-back pony called Tom, with solemn warnings from my mother to drive slowly and make sure that the milk was not disturbed by the journey. Needless to say, as soon as I got out of sight of the house, I upped Tom's travel rate to galloping mode, and hurtled down the road to Nestlé's like a charioteer from *Ben Hur*. My father often wondered why he received letters from the factory complaining that the milk delivered on such and such a date was tainted or semi-churned.

After milking, we fed the hens and the pigs and performed various other tasks, and when it was all finished, then, and only then, did we get breakfast. A young man who came to work for us at one point asked about breakfast before the work was done, and we thought that was hilariously funny – that somebody should talk about eating before the work was completed.

When we had breakfasted we walked a mile and a half to school and at the end of the day we walked the mile and a half back home. We then did our homework, but we also did all the chores again – milked the cows, fed the hens and so on; we even boiled great three-legged pots of potatoes over an open fire in what was euphemistically referred to as the Boiler Room, and, of course, we cleaned out the byres. I could give lessons on cleaning out byres.

In case there should be any misunderstanding about the seriousness of our responsibilities, a notice posted on a board on the kitchen wall listed the duties that each member of the family was expected to carry out each day, and sitting behind the notice board was a newly cut sally rod as a reminder of the penalty for non-compliance.

It was a tough but fairly simple life, but three years after we arrived in Omagh the Second World War started, and that changed everything. Only the river separated us from the training depot of the Inniskilling Fusiliers, so war and soldiers were never far away from us. If you rose in the morning and found a platoon of soldiers brewing up on your front lawn, you simply ate your breakfast and set off for school. On the way, you could run into a convoy of tanks or of army trucks blocking your path, so you stood patiently by the wayside and waited until they had passed.

As you passed the training ground on your way to or from school, you could see groups of earnest young trainees crouching among the nettle beds as they tried to conceal themselves from the enemy forces on the far side of the battlefield; and their language as they told us to f**k off and stop giving away their location to the enemy was not something we were used to hearing at school, or at home.

If the army was practising with mortars, we stayed out of the back fields, for inexperienced marksmen could overshoot the river and blow holes a yard wide in the hillside. And when they had finished, a Colonel-Blimpish figure on a white horse toured the fields and counted the holes for compensation purposes – half a crown for each hole, if memory serves me. We also went round the fields when the colonel had gone, collecting the fins and the spent shells as souvenirs. What we did not anticipate was that a neighbouring schoolboy would slip in and collect a live shell and take it home on the carrier of his bicycle. He tried to dismantle it at the back of his house with a hammer. Parts of him were found freakish distances away.

Because of the proximity of the training ground to our home, some of the exercises inevitably spilled over onto our land, with unexpected consequences. My sisters, reasonably enough, felt free to wander through the fields in their spare time, but they took no account of the mischievous, if not predatory, instincts of some of the military trainees across the river, so when a group of soldiers suddenly appeared on their side of the river and began pursuing them with menacing howls and sexual suggestions, they took to their heels and arrived home in a state of physical and emotional exhaustion.

It took a lot of diplomatic activity and delicate negotiation before a working solution was finally achieved, but from that moment onwards, the war ceased to be a diversion and became, in one way or another, a threat to all of us.

The soldiers across the way from us were always an ongoing anxiety, but a more permanent problem came with the military personnel who were billeted on our home for the duration – whether we liked it or not. At that time our household consisted of my father and mother and eight children, all under twelve years of age. Nonetheless we had to give up two substantial rooms and a share in our only bathroom, to accommodate the lodgers.

At one point a captain and his wife were imposed upon us, but from the start, for one reason or another, the chemistry between us was not good. It would be fair to say that my father was not the most patient of men. He found it hard to wait in line in his own house to use the only bathroom, and the captain's lady could spend a fair bit of time bathing and putting on make-up. It all came to a head one morning with some dispute over breakages, which finished up with the lady rushing up the stairs in tears to tell her husband how badly she had been treated. Next moment we heard the thunder of footsteps running down the stairs and the captain burst into the kitchen, his face covered in shaving lather, a towel round his neck, and wielding a very frightening cut-throat razor in his hand. It did not come to blows, but as you can imagine, everyone walked on eggshells from then onwards.

I came fourth in the family, and my twin sisters and two others followed shortly afterwards. That led to a certain level of domestic congestion, which was eventually resolved by deporting me to my granny's house outside Pettigo at the age of four. My granny was advanced in years, and domestic matters were handled by my Auntie Peg, a disciplinarian of the old school, so I tried to stay out of her way as best I could. I even attended the local primary school but I was greatly disappointed to discover that I was not allowed to go to school in my bare feet like the rest of the pupils. At that time and in that neighbourhood, deprivation was a badge of honour, and even led one scholar to complain that the rest of the pupils had patches on their clothes whereas he had none.

At this point in my development, I tended to follow my instincts rather than school discipline, and on one occasion I joined up with a passing farmer who was driving a herd of cows to market. The alarm was eventually raised, and I was returned under escort to my place of learning.

Shortly afterwards my granny died and I was returned to the bosom of my family, where, apparently, I continued to disrupt the peace and quiet of domestic life. We had no neighbours to play with, so we played with one another, and we also fought with one another, for no apparent reason. It just seemed to be the done thing at the time, to fight with your big sister.

Times were tough, benefits were non-existent and ten hungry mouths had to be fed, so we employed a man from Donegal called Joe, through the hiring fair in Omagh, to help with the farm work. I am sure it must have been a tough and lonely life for him. He had a bedroom off the kitchen which he tried to maintain as his private and personal quarters, but we children were never too observant of the rules. We poked our noses into every nook and cranny of his life and allowed the family dog to wander in and out of his bedroom unhindered, giving rise to the memorable denunciation by Joe that he could not possibly maintain a clean and tidy environment as long as 'that wee dawg was pisseen and shiteen all over the flure'.

Joe was what would now be called an illegal alien, or at least there was some technical objection to his working in the North. However, it was not his agricultural expertise but his pipe smoking that eventually led to his downfall. While having a quiet smoke in the barn one evening, he must have dropped a spark into the hay where it smouldered for some time before eventually bursting into flames that set the entire building alight. The fire brigade was called but they were not the highly scientific organisation we expect today. The pipes were duly connected to the only source of water, the River Strule, four hundred metres away, but when the pumps were turned on, the pipes were found to be back to front. By the time they got water onto the fire, the barn was a raging inferno. Joe maintained a very low profile throughout the crisis, in case someone in authority should question his bona fides, and shortly afterwards he returned to Donegal on a permanent basis.

I attended the infant school in Omagh, where I learned the valuable lesson that small women, and especially small women teachers, are a force to be reckoned with. Nothing in the intervening sixty years has caused me to revise this opinion.

I then graduated onto the Christian Brothers Primary School in Omagh, where various forms of unorthodox punishment were practised, including the application of a leather strap to the bare bottoms of offenders. Parents were fully aware of the practice, but never, to my knowledge, complained. If the civil authorities of the day were still flogging criminals and hanging women on a regular basis, it was assumed that lesser forms of physical punishment were acceptable in other walks of life.

Regardless of their legendary reputation for discipline and violence I found the Christian Brothers no more menacing than their lay colleagues, some of whom had the sense of humour of a coffin when it came to their professional life. A measure of eccentricity may have worked its way into the teaching methods of some of the staff – such as Brother Byrne's tendency to bounce hurling balls off the back wall of the classroom in the hope of keeping his pupils awake, and at least marginally involved in their lessons, though nemesis eventually overtook him when he reversed too far for his run-up and crashed into the Sacred Heart lamp, setting what little hair he had on fire. The practice of reciting the Litany of Our Lady each evening at the end of class was well intentioned but doomed to failure by the monotony of the responses. While Brother O'Connell invoked our 'Mother most amiable, Mother most admirable, etc.', the pupils responded with a mechanical 'Pray for us', until the day he stopped without warning. The class continued 'Pray for us, Pray for us', until he halted the loudest offender with a swift blow from a schoolbag.

I then progressed to the Christian Brothers Secondary School, and because I had made good progress in primary school, I was allowed to skip over first year and begin with second year. In the course of my first year there, my mother was informed by an interfering clerical uncle that if I wished to become a priest of the

Derry Diocese, I would have to go to St Columb's College and study Greek, conditions which later both proved to be false. Without further ado, I was packed off to Derry to board in St Columb's College, a military-style institution which I cordially hated, and where I started in first year, adding another two years to my miserable schooldays.

Initiation into the student community was achieved by a ceremony called 'ducking', which involved being dragged by a couple of the senior pupils to a cold tap outside the toilets and held under until you were well and truly 'ducked'. Physical punishment was endemic to every department of school life. If you spoke when you were expected to remain silent, you were slapped on the hand with a leather strap. If you gave the wrong answer to a sum in the maths class, you were slapped; if you ran where you should walk, you were slapped; if you omitted any portion of your homework or even misspelt a word in your English essay, you were slapped. One of the maths teachers introduced his own unique and highly unjust method of punishment. He perched on one of the desks in the front row and announced to the pupils on either side of him, 'If I see somebody misbehaving, I have no intention of rising from here. I will hit you, and you can hit the culprit when you get him outside'.

In some matters discipline was passed into the hands of the prefects – senior pupils appointed to various degrees of authority, who could not resist the occasional temptation to illustrate their importance by punishing their juniors. On the rare occasion when we were allowed out en masse to the local cinema, some hardy souls would inevitably break ranks and sneak into the local newsagents for a packet of sweets. The punishment was swift and merciless. The offenders were rounded up as soon as we returned to college and herded into the senior library where they were beaten about the head by the prefects until they were in a state of tearful surrender, then they were warned never to dare usurp or defy in any way the instructions and the authority of the prefects.

Hunger was the other determining factor in college life. On our first evening in residence we sat down at table and ate the round and a half of loaf bread that was sitting on our plates, and then waited. My lifetime friend, Paul, eventually asked, 'I wonder what we are getting for tea?' and I answered, 'I think you have just eaten it'. And I was right. Favours could be bought for food. Hence, parcels from home were a strong factor in determining who was in favour and who was victimised. Various subterfuges to acquire food were practised by the more ruthless students, who did not hesitate to take advantage of their more innocent comrades. The ration of butter for the evening meal was two pats per pupil, whereas the morning ration was only one pat, so the thrifty souls would stick half a pat to the underside of the table, in the hope of retrieving it in the morning. The more hardened criminals simply ran their index finger along the underside of the table as soon as they arrived and scooped up the savings of their innocent comrades. Likewise, at dinner, the allocation of potatoes was one potato per person, so the more robust diners made sure that the plate of potatoes was close to hand and grabbed the biggest potato as soon as grace was finished. And in the midst of all this mayhem, my mother used to wonder that we were not taught good manners and etiquette at 'college'!

One of the few things in life that I can truthfully look back on with pride is that when – to my surprise, and that of a lot of others – I was appointed head prefect, or more commonly head boy, I abolished all punishment sessions in the library, no matter the reason, organised by prefects. And as a measure of my own unhappiness during those years in Derry, I have never, in the sixty years of life since then, attended a single reunion or any function to do with St Columb's College.

It would take too long to go into all the influences that persuaded – or pressurised – me to study for priesthood. Many years ago I came across a book written by a group of priests outlining their reasons for joining the priesthood. I thought, 'at last, a chance to see where I fit into this exotic way of life', but the book was a miserable failure. It simply rambled around the circumstances of each individual vocation but never really got to grips with the central question. I make no pretence at providing sound and reasonable motives for becoming a priest myself, but I do know that in our house, 'Why did you become a priest?' was the wrong question. For us the question was, 'Why can you not become a priest?' We were taught that we were privileged to belong to the Body of Christ, when so many deserving souls were deprived of that privilege, and we were silently asked, 'Is there any reason why you cannot take that message and that privilege of the faith to the multitudes that have been deprived of it?'

Faith was a big factor in our family life. Prayers at night consisted of the Rosary, Litany, and prayers of petition and intercession for all kinds of purposes – ranging from everything, from the foreign missions to the cousin who would be having surgery in the morning. Morning prayers were personal (but no less obligatory) to every member of the family. As soon as you descended into the kitchen, you dropped on your knees and said your prayers.

Mass on Sunday was always first Mass. If it was at eight o'clock you went to the eight o'clock Mass. If, as happened on Christmas morning, the first Mass was at six o'clock, we went to that one.

Confession every Saturday night was obligatory. We all piled into the Morris Eight, drove to the Sacred Heart Church in Omagh and confessed our sins. The only hiccup I can recall was when the priest threw me out of the confession box – not literally, but he issued a threat – 'Are you going to get out or do I have to come round and throw you out?' – that was equally compelling. It would appear that children's confessions were timetabled for the morning; since I lived in 'the country', I had to go in the evening with my parents, but that was not considered adequate justification by my confessor. I got as far as: 'Bless me Father, for I have sinned…', before a disembodied voice said, 'get out'. I thought he must be talking to the penitent on the other side of the box, so I started again, 'Bless me Father, for I have sinned', and this time he issued his ultimatum, 'are you going to get out or do I have to come round and throw you out?' My mother had a very tricky time explaining away his erratic behaviour, without condemning him roundly for a bad-tempered gulpin.

Priesthood was not a privilege. It was a sacrifice. If God has been so good to you, how are you going to repay him? So we set our sights on this way of life that was not necessarily attractive but which comforted us that we were doing the will of God and maybe even fulfilling our destiny. Only this kind of heroism could have persuaded us to forego the high life and entertainment that our contemporaries were enjoying. They were going to dances, dating girls and staying out late at night, whereas we were locked up in a military-style institution, forbidden a lot of the time even to speak to one another, allowed home only twice a year and even then, curtailed from any normal social intercourse by our black suits and white shirts, which we were compelled to wear at all times. We were taught to make sacrifices, and studying for the priesthood was definitely a sacrifice. But even then it was not our choice. You or I might decide that we wanted to be a priest, but unless a bishop called you to be a priest you were going nowhere. There was, I remember, a total of sixteen candidates for priesthood in the Derry Diocese the year I applied. We were all summoned one Saturday morning to St Columb's College where a panel of senior clergy interviewed us all, and eventually decided to accept eight of us and to reject the other eight. No reasons were given.

After St Columb's, I went to Maynooth, another military-style institution, where we rose at six o'clock in the morning and went to bed at ten o'clock at night, and were not allowed to speak between half past eight at night and eight o'clock in the morning – and that included anyone we might happen to share a room with. We were simply not allowed to speak to one another. It was called the solemn silence, and during those hours, any infringement was punishable by immediate expulsion.

On first arrival, we were given a number which determined our priority in every activity from then until ordination. In the lecture hall, we were seated numerically and the professor could consult his list and determine who was not paying suitable attention in row D. Nobody knew our names. I can guarantee that no one who taught me any subject in my three years in Maynooth would have been able to put a name on me if he met me in the street, even in my student days.

I expected to find a high degree of tolerance and understanding from those whose responsibility was to prepare us for the priestly life, but I quickly learned that the more exalted their qualification for their particular task, the touchier they were about defending their status. I foolishly believed that you could bring forward arguments for and against a certain point of view and that your opponent – be he pupil or professor – would be willing to give due consideration to your suggestions. Sadly, it did not work out that way. The Greek professor, who hailed from Kerry or some other Celtic outback, claimed that his interpretation of a certain paragraph from Dean Swift was the obvious and reasonable interpretation, whereas I insisted that there was an alternative and even more compelling interpretation, but he could not be persuaded. So that night, I went to the university library and consulted the *Shorter Oxford English Dictionary* – both massive volumes – and discovered that the passage from Dean Swift was quoted as an example of the meaning that I had given to it. I duly carried the results of my research into the Greek class the next day, and was grudgingly acknowledged as having found the right interpretation, but when it came to exam results I paid dearly. Even though I had excelled in Greek studies, and had even written Greek essays – away and beyond the call of duty – I was given a pass in my degree, while everyone else was given honours; but then, the Lord works in mysterious ways. After ordination, all my colleagues who had excelled in their degree results were sent to teach in various institutions, the last thing on earth I wanted, whereas I was sent to a quiet country parish!

Maynooth was also noted for its exotic variety of rules and regulations. You could be expelled for eating sweets or reading newspapers, but you could smoke all day if you wanted to. I know you will want a reason for this erratic behaviour. Basically, the rules in Maynooth, I am told, were written before smoking was commonplace and they were never updated. Foodstuffs, on the other hand, inevitably attracted vermin, so sweets were outlawed.

Rules were so strict and their application so stringent that a student, who found himself locked into the bathroom on the fourth floor one morning, tried to climb down a drainpipe in order to appear punctually at morning prayer, and fell three floors to the ground. It ended his clerical career, and probably many other openings in life that he might have pursued.

I could handle the academic end of things without much difficulty, but on the diplomatic front I failed miserably. It almost seemed that the authorities were more intent on weeding out everyone with any trace of human fallibility rather than trying to encourage us to overcome our weaknesses and to learn to communicate with the rest of the human race.

After three years in Maynooth, I was told that I was being sent to Rome to study, along with a few other Derry students. Many years later, Bishop Farren explained to me why I was sent to Rome: 'Either you went to Rome or you would have been expelled from Maynooth'. It would appear that the authorities in Maynooth did not sympathise with my outlook on priestly training; or maybe there was a rogue gene in the family, because my younger brother was duly expelled from Maynooth some years later. He made the mistake of keeping a diary, which the dean of discipline read while my brother was attending morning prayer, in which his opinion of the dean of discipline was a bit too candidly expressed.

Anyway, in the year 1956, we set out overland for Rome, dressed in our black suits, white shirts, black ties and black socks, and inevitably someone asked us what the uniform was all about. 'We are apprentice undertakers on our way to a conference in Paris,' we answered. We thought we were being very streetwise. Nobody believed a word of it, of course. Anyway, our responses gave a fair indication to the world at large how smart we were. We had been nowhere, had met no foreigners, wore our uniforms without question, knew nothing, and I mean nothing, about women, and were going to bring salvation to the ends of the earth. For that was how the bishop and his minions had outlined priestly vocation. We had committed our lives to God, so whatever he said, through his representatives on earth, was okay with us. Only later did we learn that God was a lot easier to negotiate with than bishops.

From the day we were accepted as candidates for the priesthood, we donned our black suits and henceforth we never appeared in public without them. If you went to the seaside for a holiday, you wore your black suit. If you went to a football match, you wore your black suit; and because you had to wear your black suit, there were places you could not go. You could not go to a pub, but then pubs were a rarity, and your presence would have been interpreted as irrefutable evidence that you were not cut out for priesthood. You could not go to a dance hall. The very idea of a clerical student in a dance hall was a contradiction in terms. If you were seen walking down the street with a reasonably good-looking girl, you could bet there would be some shrivelled old biddy on the phone with the bishop before you got home. You were a candidate for priesthood, the highest honour. If you trifled with the rules and regulations, you were out. And there were plenty of other candidates to take your place.

In the course of the four years I spent in Rome, I was allowed home only once. In the other years, we were sent to a Mediterranean villa for three months during the summer break, where we spent our days eating whatever was available – and remember that this was post-war rationing time – and the rest of the time sleeping and swimming. It was the most utterly boring time of my life. Instead of letting us home and allowing us to get jobs in a shop or a factory where we might meet other people and learn something about human nature, the official thinking was that we should be screened off from the rest of the world and protected from all the sinful influences that pervaded daily life. In short, we finished up experts in Greek and canon law and knew absolutely nothing about ordinary men and women.

I was ordained in St John Lateran's Basilica in Rome on 12 March 1960. The ordination ceremony began at seven o'clock in the morning with what were called minor orders and, finally, at about midday we were ordained to the priesthood. It was a feat of endurance rather than a liturgical triumph.

We hung around Rome for another three months, supposedly studying or doing courses, but most of our time was spent meandering around Rome visiting churches and museums, or sampling the various restaurants or beer houses in the neighbourhood.

I went home at the end of June and was mercifully spared the bonfires and the band parades that other newly ordained priests had to endure. A priest from the parish was big business in those days. I spent almost two months wandering around the locality, waiting patiently for some kind of permanent appointment. It never came, and one day I ran into my friend Scotchy McKean, also newly ordained, but from a different diocese. He had just volunteered for five years of missionary work in Peru, and with the careful consideration and long-term planning that characterised all our decisions in those days he said to me, 'Why don't you come with me?' And with equally long and careful consideration I replied, 'Why not?'

Next day we drove to Derry and, while Scotchy entertained himself with the sights and sounds of the Maiden City, I ascended the stairs to Bishop Farren's sitting room and I made my pitch without preamble or explanation: 'My Lord, can I go to Peru for five years?' You have to understand that Bishop Farren had led a very sheltered life. He was a teacher before he became bishop and he was used to giving orders and having them obeyed without question. Small talk to put you at your ease, enquiries about your general health and well-being, careful examination of your query before answering, dissecting the pros and cons of the matter before reaching a decision – these were not part of his culture. On this occasion he simply said, 'Certainly not', and sent me to Coleraine the following day.

Whenever I reminisce about Coleraine, I find that Tarquin is much better remembered than myself. My parish priest was a very mild-mannered man who believed, with good reason, in my estimation, that curates were an incompetent and inexperienced group of innocents who should never be entrusted with anything involving discretion or responsibility without strict supervision. An early example that caught my attention was his insistence that only on a Saturday night, under his personal supervision, should we enter in the register the baptisms that we had performed.

Tarquin was a boxer pup which a friend gave me shortly after I arrived in Coleraine. He was about eight weeks old and cute as button, and my housekeeper adopted him. After chores every evening, she sat in the kitchen rocking back and forth with Tarquin in her lap, which was a very touching and homely sight when he was eight weeks old. When he was eight months, however, it looked ridiculous. Here was this diminutive young lady with a huge boxer dog on her knee, blissfully petting and stroking him as though it were the most normal thing in the world. Sadly, there was nothing normal about Tarquin. He was a brainless lunatic with outrageously destructive tendencies. No attempts at cajoling, bribing or threatening him made any difference. He moved through the neighbourhood like the hordes of Genghis Khan on a bad hair day, leaving a trail of terror and destruction. It was not that he lacked sociability or an affection for people. Children especially he loved, but his gestures of affection were so violent that he left a trail of grazed and muddied children behind him, which in turn gave way to a trail of vengeful mothers looking for the owner's blood.

Nervous adults were equally vulnerable. On one occasion I took him to visit the local convent and as usual he set off to explore the neighbourhood and meet the neighbours. Piercing shrieks soon informed me that he had found them. When we eventually tracked him down, he was sitting in front of a terror-stricken nun, wondering why she was backed up against a concrete wall and screaming her head off. She had evidently mistaken his exuberant greeting for a savage attack. On the domestic front he was not any more disciplined. As myself and my fellow curate sat at lunch one day, Tarquin appeared at the window, put his feet on the sill and looked around the room. The other curate foolishly, or perhaps deliberately, called on Tarquin to come in, emphasising his words with inviting gestures and sounds. Tarquin simply took two steps backwards and came straight through the window – glass and all.

He was arrested on several occasions by the Royal Ulster Constabulary for physically molesting young people, male and female. Their parents were reasonable people but when the children consistently arrived home with muddied faces and tattered school uniforms, the parents decided the time had come to take a stand. An ultimatum was issued. Either he would be transferred to another parish where his craziness would have more scope, or he would be transferred to another owner who might control his erratic behaviour more effectively by a regime of care and discipline. But neither alternative worked. I took him with me to a new parish but he was soon seen disappearing over the horizon in pursuit of a heavily pregnant lady who was screaming at the top of her voice, 'Call off your dog, call off your dog!'

That was the Parish of Faughanvale, where I moved after two years in Coleraine, to be curate to the only ninety-year-old active parish priest in the diocese. He had a reputation for holiness, but if you live long enough that is fairly easy to acquire. He spoke as if he were perpetually contending with a badly fitting set of false teeth, which he probably was, snapping them together at the end of each word to prevent them shooting across the floor.

I arrived on a snowy winter evening, and was puzzled to find a line of men and women standing outside the sacristy door of the church. Later enquiries revealed that these were penitents waiting patiently to get to confession, but no one could offer any reason why they were compelled to stand outside in the snow rather than line up in the church and enter the sacristy from there. I tried to persuade the parish priest that a confession box inside the church might be a good investment, but he dismissed the idea out of hand, so in due course I went ahead and installed a confession box without his permission.

Needless to say, it almost led to a declaration of war. He burst into my room after Mass and demanded to know who had authorised me to erect a confession box in his church. So I told him that if he were willing to sit down and talk about the matter, I would be very happy to oblige. Instead he dropped to his knees beside me and called upon God to witness the flagrant disobedience of this young curate, before launching into a solo rendition of the Rosary. He persevered for the first decade, but when it became obvious that he was not going to make much headway – especially since I continued watching Z-Cars on the TV while he was praying – he called it a day. After that we got on quite well. It seemed to clear the air, but you had to be alert for the outlandish plans that he would occasionally conjure up without telling anyone.

He slept anywhere, at any time, as the inclination took him, but most of the night was spent wandering restlessly around the house. On my first night in residence, he arrived in my bedroom at about half past two in the morning and delivered a dissertation on some subject that I was completely unable to interpret, but since it was the middle of the night I assumed that it was a crisis of some kind. I duly rose and got dressed, but when I went in search of the parish priest, he was nowhere to be found. I roused the housekeeper, who was more used to these midnight encounters, and without comment she escorted me to the parish priest's bedroom where he was fast asleep. It was her way of saying, 'Get used to it. Nobody knows what is coming next!'

One of our first joint operations was a funeral where the deceased had indicated his desire to be buried with his mother and father in the family grave. I only became aware of this when the gravedigger set a large hessian bag full of bones and pieces of timber at the side of the grave. When the coffin was lowered into the grave, the bag was solemnly upended and the contents emptied with a resounding rattle on top of the coffin. On enquiry, I was told that these were the bones and the remainder of the coffins of mother and father which had been unceremoniously excavated from the grave to make room for their son. Apparently, it was not an unusual practice, stemming from the early days of the local workhouse, where to this day a large inscription across the gable of what used to be the dining room is preserved: '*The Rattling of the Bones*'.

The parish priest designed an extension to the house, but unfortunately he never anticipated the need for accurate measurements and workable levels. He built a bedroom extension, but when he broke through the walls to join up with the existing structure, he discovered the adjoining floors were two feet apart and the doorways in the wrong place. As a consequence, he had to build a most intricate set of stairs to connect the two structures. As it happened, his curate at the time was a man of humour and imagination, and he pinned a notice at the bottom of the stairs: 'Bends for half a mile'.

His erratic sleep patterns were not confined to the parochial house. On one occasion, he went to attend an old friend who was ill and was duly escorted into the sick room, but when he had not reappeared two hours later, the lady of the house grew alarmed and went upstairs to see what had happened. At first glance, she could see nothing in the room but the patient sleeping peacefully. On further investigation, however, she discovered the missing clergyman on the far side of the bed, fast asleep on the floor.

He believed firmly in the good old days and the good old ways of doing things. For example he would occasionally announce a concert in the parish hall. No mention was ever made of performers, but when the audience had finally gathered, he would mount the stage and call on members of the audience to come up and sing or recite or display whatever talents they possessed.

Even such a straightforward task as reading out the priest's collection took on a new twist. He added a running commentary so that the final results sounded something like: 'John Smith, half a crown. Are you sure you can manage it? William Jones, ten shillings. I thought the sheep would have done better than that, Willie. Patrick White, three pounds. Now, there's a man who knows the price of coal' His control over the congregation was absolute. On one occasion he was warned that the gallery in his outlying church was dangerous and, indeed, was liable to collapse without warning if immediate repairs were not carried out. This suggestion that something old might be defective touched a sore point with him. So, on Sunday morning, when Mass was finished, he told the women and children in the congregation to leave and then ordered all the men into the gallery. 'Now', he said, 'when I say jump, I want everyone to jump'. And jump they did. Not over the gallery but up and down, thus proving to his complete satisfaction that however old the gallery, it was still safe for generations to come. The possibility of it wiping out a generation of the congregation in one fell swoop never seemed to have crossed his mind.

He had a firm belief in the power of the priest and never hesitated to threaten dissenters or troublemakers with the 'curse of God' when they stepped out of line. Needless to say, word quickly spread that he could really wield the power of God in his defence, until it reached not only his own flock but that of the local Reformed minister. One of his farming fraternity had words with the parish priest, but when his livestock began to sicken and die – by coincidence surely – the pastor's reputation spread like wildfire.

His nephew lodged in the parochial house and drove him wherever he wanted to go in his broken-down 1936 Austin Sixteen. On one occasion, however, a stray cow stepped into his path and severely damaged the Austin. The parish priest was slightly shaken up, but the neighbours rushed to escort him into the nearest dwelling, where he was given generous helpings of restorative whiskey while the nephew and the Royal Ulster Constabulary dealt with questions of responsibility for the cow and the car. The cow was released unconditionally, but the car was impounded and strict orders given that it could not be reclaimed until a qualified mechanic declared it roadworthy. The parish priest learned this only when he returned home later, and in fairly trenchant language he declared that no policeman, and especially no member of the RUC, was going to tell him what he could or could not do with his car, and announced his intention of going straight to the barracks and getting the car back.

By this time I had run out of patience, so I told him that he was going nowhere and, if necessary, I would use physical force to prevent him. Which is precisely what I had to do. It finished with the parish priest clinging to the door jambs with both arms while I tried to prise them apart by putting both my own arms around his stomach and pulling backwards with all my strength, and at the same time trying to avoid the vicious kicks that were directed at my legs by the heel of the his boot. Eventually, sheer exhaustion brought things to a close. The parish priest sat down on a chair, breathing heavily, and then he started to laugh. 'Ye bate me', he said, 'ye bate me'.

He used to take his holidays in Donegal and was an enthusiastic exponent of the merits of sea bathing. Even though his doctor had warned him of the possible damage to his heart and lungs, and even when his bathing trunks were confiscated, and even after he had been deprived of the tools for cobbling together any makeshift bathing trunks, he still took his bath in the sea, only this time he wore absolutely nothing. It was then that a fairly sedate English couple called at the house and informed the housekeeper that they were worried about 'the old gentleman', because he had just passed them on the beach, running as hard as he could, absolutely naked, patting his chest and muttering to himself: 'That'll show them, that'll show them'.

I was moved from Faughanvale to Iskaheen in February 1964. I was twenty-seven years of age, three years ordained and completely, as they say, 'wet behind the ears'. My earliest and most vivid memory there is the occasion when I very nearly burned the parochial house to the ground. I lit a fire in an unused fireplace, and only when the smoke began coming down the chimney instead of up did I realise there was a blockage somewhere. So I got a ladder, climbed up to the chimney top and found a large crow's nest. I shifted it as much as I could but the crow was obviously taking no chances and had built a solid foundation, so I got a fence post and tried hammering the nest downwards into the fireplace. Needless to say, the crow was way ahead of me. So I resorted to extreme measures. I got a can of petrol, poured a large quantity down the chimney and tossed a lighted match after it. I had just got my nose out of the way when a pillar of fire shot into the air. It didn't burn the house down but there were lots of strange crackling noises before it settled down. And these were the days when the priest knew everything!

My parish priest at the time was a simple man and in many ways the ideal parish priest, for he let you get on with whatever you were doing without interference. He didn't welcome change. When told that the Vatican Council had ruled that all new churches – and he had just finished building one – would have the altar facing the people, his response was not: 'Oh, why did we not know it earlier', but rather, 'Thank God we got it finished in time'. He lambasted the entire congregation one Sunday morning for what he described as an orgy of wine, women and song that he had witnessed in Muff over the weekend. I was impressed by the look of disappointment on the face of some of the young men in the pews, thinking that they too were appalled at the lowering of standards in the locality, until further experience told me that their disappointment stemmed from the fact that there had been an orgy of wine, women and song in Muff, and they knew nothing about it. In fact, the nearest we ever got to wine, women and song was the weekend dances in Borderland, the commercial dance hall in

Muff, and in St Mary's, the local parochial hall. It was my responsibility, I was told, to stand in the doorway of St Mary's and make sure that the more enthusiastic supporters of the alcohol business were kept out, and that the equally enthusiastic supporters of other forms of recreation were kept in. I was not always successful.

I tried to provide alternative entertainments in the parish hall and set up a boxing club for the young men of the district. We bought gloves and punchballs to get things off the ground, and with adequate supervision on the first night, we practised some of the more fundamental boxing activities; but without supervision on the second night the punchballs were ripped from their moorings and the boxing gloves were used as footballs!

Three years later, I was moved to the Altinure end of Banagher Parish. By sheer coincidence, my new parish priest was appointed at the same time as myself. His predecessor, an ardent supporter of Gaelic games, had a heart attack and died on the playing field while refereeing a match, but there was very little chance of a recurrence of such an event since the new parish priest was very limited in his organisational abilities. He was a jovial, simple man who, despite having studied in Paris for four years, could not speak a coherent word of French when I knew him. Like the road to hell, his life was paved with good intentions, but he rarely got around to implementing any of them. He constructed a state-of-the-art office in his new parochial house, but it did not improve efficiency or increase the speed at which even the most fundamental duties were carried out. Matters eventually came to a head when the newly appointed principal of the local school came to me with the complaint that she had not been paid any wages since her appointment six months previously. I asked the parish priest if he had duly registered the appointment of the principal with the Department of Education. As he always tended to do when backed into a corner, he stood upon his dignity and announced that he was the manager of the school and hence needed no one to approve his appointment. Only when I pointed out to him that unless he were willing to pay the principal's salary himself he should reach some agreement with the Department of Education did he stand down.

This crisis, however, was merely the tip of the iceberg. It soon came to light that many other administrative tasks had been neglected for no apparent reason. Eventually, I had to demand a summit meeting to discuss the source of this neglect.

To cut a long story short, I was eventually admitted into his state-of-the-art office where I discovered a mound of correspondence – approximately three feet high – in the centre of the room, that had never even been opened, much less answered, since his appointment as parish priest. Apparently, the relentless avalanche of official documents had so overwhelmed him that he eventually gave up trying, and merely tossed the mail every morning into the office and closed the door on it, until, like Topsy, the pile of unanswered mail grew and grew, and the consequences overflowed into the parish.

The unwritten law of the diocese was that you tried to resolve any problems you confronted before bringing them to the attention of the bishop, so with the help of a senior cleric we reached an agreement that, in the future, I would handle all administrative and financial matters in the parish – while giving the impression to the world at large of business as usual – and that is how we worked until the parish priest's untimely death one night, from a heart attack. A combination of inadequate medical resources, aggravated by his curate's complete ignorance of even the most fundamental CPR, speeded his demise!

If truth were told, he should never have been appointed to a position of responsibility, but it was seen as an insult if a man were not appointed as parish priest at some stage of his career. He was a most affable and friendly individual and people were extremely fond of him, but the very thought of administrative duties, or the responsibility of dealing with people in authority, terrified him. If he had to approach the bishop about any matter, he tried every subterfuge to avoid it. On one occasion, I accompanied him when we had to approach the bishop about five different matters, but once at the bishop's doorstep, he turned to me in panic. 'We'll only ask him about two of the points today and we'll come back about the others some other day.'

Ironically, everything went smoothly on that occasion, and all five points were duly covered, until, at the very end, as I was packing away my notes and documents, he reached into his trouser pocket and brought out a wrinkled sheet of paper which he duly smoothed out on the bishop's desk and said, 'I wonder, would you sign this for me, my lord?' The bishop looked at it in wonderment and eventually said, 'But there's nothing written on it'. 'Oh', said the parish priest, 'I was going to fill it in later'.

By the time the bishop finished with him on that occasion, he was a nervous wreck. He must have stopped off for a few jars of Dutch courage on the way home, for as he rounded the curve past the parochial hall, he misjudged the angle and crashed into a telegraph pole. The bingo players in the hall came rushing to his rescue, hoping that he was not too badly injured, but his only concern was: 'Don't tell Fr Collins'.

The only innovation I introduced to Altinure was camping holidays for young people. Holidays of any kind at that time were a rarity, and the thought of not merely getting away from home but getting away from home along with your friends had a lot going for it. I bought a couple of ex-army marquee tents and a batch of tent beds, and the rest of the equipment we begged or borrowed from the locals. As a precautionary measure, we decided to erect the tents the night before we left. Sure enough, when all the bits and pieces had been put together, there was still a massive six-foot gap in the side wall of one of the tents. Fortunately, I recalled seeing a large sheet of timber in a shed at the back of the church, so I cut out six feet from it and our problem was solved. Months afterwards, as we were preparing for Christmas, the sacristan, the man in charge of the church and responsible for erecting the crib, approached me with a face like thunder. 'You won't believe it, Father', he said, 'but some bastard has cut a big six-foot swathe from the floor of the new crib' I duly sympathised and passed quickly on to other matters.

Our camping skills were very basic. Hygiene, health and safety, child protection, qualified supervisors – all of these were optional extras in those days. Everyone took care of everyone else, as they did at home, and over four years we never had a casualty. The thinking was, 'if it isn't broke, don't try to fix it'.

Photography had always been a hobby of mine, and when I went to Altinure, I found both time and subject matter on my doorstep, culminating eventually in the publication of a book of photographs of a Travelling family that I took in 1969. It is something of a miracle that the negatives survived for so long.

In 1974, I went out to see my brother, who is a priest in New Zealand, and when I returned I found Bishop Daly in charge of the diocese and my name on the transfer list. I found out about the change by pure accident. I had telephoned a clerical colleague about some matter and, as I was about to ring off, he said: 'How do you think you will like the change?' 'What change?', I asked. 'Did you not know? You were changed to the Waterside?'

I moved to the Waterside in Derry and exchanged my large independent house for two rooms in a run-down house in Chapel Road. The kitchen was in the basement, and if I felt like a cup of tea, I travelled from the sitting room on the second floor to the basement kitchen where, as soon as I switched on the lights, a veritable army of large brown German cockroaches went scurrying for cover into every crack and crevice in the floor and the walls.

Serving as chaplain to Altnagelvin hospital was part of my remit in the Waterside, which meant that I could be called out for emergencies two or three times a night and then expected to handle regular duties the following day. By this time the Troubles were in full swing and I was quickly introduced to the trauma and the grief they could generate. In the country areas, the survivors of the 1920s retold the stories of the Civil War, but the young men had no plan but to make trouble for the powers, that be in any way they could. In my parish they started by blowing up the local sewage plant – the only productive industry in the neighbourhood, as one cynic put it – and then moved on to the lorries of the Forestry Department. Sadly, they did not stop there. While most non-Catholics regarded membership of the UDR as a convenient source of extra income, Catholics regarded the regiment as the enemy of the people, and before long, the hardworking farmer who had previously set off to drill and train in the evenings without a qualm had to face the real possibility of lethal attacks by a vicious and hidden enemy.

Sadly, that is how it happened in my parish. An industrious local farmer, a member of the UDR, was ambushed in his own farmyard and shot dead. No one knew for sure who had done it, but all the usual suspects were rounded up and interned, and from then on, both sides launched a useless war of words and an equally worthless war on the ground, without regard for the victims. It affected everybody. One young man from the parish tried to set off a bomb to wipe out his enemies, and instead blew himself up. Another found himself facing a lifetime in jail even though he had done nothing but buy a car that I used to drive. I had exchanged it with a dealer for a new car and the dealer had sold it on to a gentleman with definite Republican tendencies. I was woken about six months later at five o'clock in the morning by the police asking if I was the owner of a Ford Corsair 2000E car, registration number such and such. They had stopped a group of men in it on Craigavon Bridge in Derry in the middle of the night and were anxious to know my connection. I duly explained that I had sold the car to a dealer many months earlier, but they made much of the fact that I was still the registered owner of the car. Some weeks later, I heard on the radio that a leading member of the Provisional IRA had been stopped and arrested by the Garda in Donegal while driving the same car.

I heard nothing further until a young man from the parish arrived on my doorstep several months later in a very agitated state. He had bought the same car when it was returned to the dealer, but when he started to dismantle it for renovation, he found a belt of armour-piercing bullets hidden in the panel of the driver's door. He knew that if this cargo were discovered at any checkpoint, he would not see the daylight for a long time. It took a lot of high-level negotiation, involving the great and the good on the political front, but eventually an agreement was reached, whereby the ammunition would be handed over to the police and the young man would be allowed him to keep his car without penalty.

The Troubles affected everybody, every day. The shortest journey, the quietest village, the most harmless of people were all subject to harassment and sometimes to violence. As I sat in my house in the foothills of the Sperrins one day, I heard three mysterious crumps in the distance, but paid little heed until a panic-stricken parishioner arrived with the news that three bombs had exploded in the neighbouring village of Claudy. By the time I got there, the village was a shambles of smoke and rubble and no one knew how many were dead or wounded, but even those who had survived were in a dreadful state. Many of them were my parishioners and worked in the village, but they knew only too well that it was only by the grace of God that they too were not among the casualties.

The most innocent of activities could lead to disaster. I used to take a group of young people to perform at local concerts or to compete in talent competitions, and on one particular occasion ,six of us – two adults and four children – were returning in triumph from a competition where everyone had won at least one prize, when we noticed a car behind us flashing its lights. We thought it was someone from our locality who knew my car or some supporters of the talent competition, and paid little attention. In normal times we would have stopped to investigate, but shortly before this, it had been reported in the news that a couple returning from a night out had been flashed down in similar fashion and when they stopped, they were robbed of their car and their belongings, so we decided to keep driving until we reached the security of our own village. However, as we approached a very twisted bridge we had to slow down – the other car closed up behind us, and only then did we hear the police siren, so we stopped on the bridge. The other car pulled up behind us and two policemen and two military policemen, all carrying machine guns, jumped out shouting, 'Put your hands in the air!' The four children were terrified and did not move, but I and the lady who was helping me stumbled out and stood with our backs to the police with our hands on the roof of the car while we were patted up and down and our pockets searched; in the meantime the military police climbed into the car and began to interrogate the children.

For the next two hours, we were harangued and questioned, but no answers that we gave were satisfactory, no documents that we produced were acceptable, and not even the fact that I was wearing full clerical gear could convince them that I was who I claimed to be. A passing motorist was questioned and he identified me immediately, but it made no difference. They stood us by the roadside while the children sat crying in the car, and eventually they announced that since they could not make radio contact with their headquarters, two of them would drive to a place with better reception and check out our credentials.

They returned about fifteen minutes later and solemnly informed us that their superiors could not identify anyone of my name or description living in this neighbourhood, and that consequently they were placing me under arrest, and would I kindly come with them. I told them that I had taken these children from their homes earlier in the evening, and their parents expected me to deliver them safely back to their homes, without exception, and consequently, until I had done this I was going nowhere. Inevitably, there was further argument until eventually, as a compromise, I suggested that if they wanted to follow me, they could witness the return of the children to their homes, and then follow me to my house where I would present incontrovertible evidence that I was who I was claiming to be, and they could take it from there. At my house, they examined the unopened post lying in the hallway and the photographs of me hanging on the walls, and eventually departed, at last satisfied that we were not part of some hitherto unknown terrorist group. Next day, I reported the incident to the chief of police in Derry, and he was duly apologetic, but gave the distinct impression that there were some things he could influence and other things that he could not.

When I moved to the Waterside in Derry in 1974, things got worse. A young man from my previous parish had married and moved there. He lived in a quiet area where the different cultures seemed to get on quite well together, but he worked for an Irish language organisation called Gael Linn, and inevitably there were those who regarded anything to do with the Irish language as a cover for Republican activities. One evening he answered his doorbell and was shot dead at point-blank range on his own doorstep. The parish hall was burned to the ground and some time later, I was caught up in a car bomb that exploded about fifty metres from my own doorstep. Life was always tense and complicated. If you wanted to go over to the city side, you allowed at least an hour – and maybe more – to get you through all the checkpoints and delays that were a part of the half-mile journey.

Four years later, I was moved to Long Tower, perhaps better known as the Bogside, where the same kind of carnage continued for the next seventeen years. It is very hard to convey the chaotic nature of clerical life during that period. The Troubles monopolised the time and the energies of the priest in one way or another. On the very day I took up office in Long Tower, a man arrived at the parochial house to report that he thought someone was being held captive in the church. When I got there I found a pale and nervous-looking individual flanked on either side by a pair of burly looking escorts, all of them apparently deeply immersed in prayer. I could get no satisfactory explanation for their sudden and unlikely conversion to the art of meditation, but when I insisted that I would not have the church used as a temporary guardhouse ,they eventually left.

The unwritten agreement, or so I thought, with the various paramilitary groups, was that the church and its grounds were sacrosanct, but they had no hesitation about using them if it suited their purposes. On one occasion, I had just concluded a requiem Mass for a Republican supporter, and as I made my way back to the sacristy to change into my street clothes before going to the cemetery for the burial, I heard a volley of shots behind me. It took me completely by surprise, for there was a huge police presence outside the church – someone counted seventy-two police Landrovers alone – and I could not fathom how someone had smuggled guns into the church grounds right under their eyes. I later learned how gullible I was. They had smuggled the guns into the church the previous night and hidden them in my confession box. Their familiarity with their faith did not convince them that what they were doing was a desecration of the house of God, but it was sufficiently detailed to inform them that there were unlikely to be too many requests for confession on the morning of a Republican funeral.

Inevitably, there were repercussions. That evening I told the bishop that I was taking a few days off, for I was exhausted, and impressed on him the importance of taking no action on this matter until we had time to sit down and think our plans through. However, pressure from all quarters was brought to bear on the bishop and he capitulated by announcing that in the future, requiem Mass would be denied to those responsible for violent deaths in the Troubles, though they would still be given a Christian burial. I heard the announcement on the evening news and I returned from my break in a highly inflamed state of mind. The bishop's argument was that funerals without requiem Mass were commonplace, so that it did not constitute a major departure from common practice; but needless to say the Republican movement saw it as political and religious discrimination against their members. From that moment onwards, funerals became a nightmare.

They were, however, merely part of the problem. Nothing was foreseeable, nothing predictable. For example, a highly respected Catholic community policeman, originally from the Republic of Ireland, was ambushed as he left his workplace. Something like forty bullets were sprayed over his car, yet he escaped unscathed; but his son told me forty years later that he had never really recovered from the event.

An incident in the local secondary school caused eyebrows to be raised. A pupil arrived in school one morning in an apparently advanced state of pregnancy, only to be exposed by an experienced vice-principal who hefted her upper garment into the air and sent a cascade of bullets flying all over the assembly hall.

When a cache of mortars and grenades was found in a disused storage facility by a leader of the youth club, the local curate worked out an arrangement whereby the offending material would be delivered to the police, and that would be the end of the matter. In due course, he and another curate loaded the explosives into the parish bus and drove it to a riverside car park which had been cleared for the occasion. On the principle that ignorance is bliss, they cheerfully barrelled into the car park with their load of contraband and handed it over to the authorities. Only later, I think, when they recalled the frantic dive for cover by the waiting police escort, did the danger of the whole operation occur to them.

Death and destruction did not necessarily occur as a consequence of the action of one side upon the other. Sometimes actions were taken against members of their own side. These could be even more harrowing than those inflicted by the enemy. I remember one young man, extremely tall, about six foot four, flaming red hair, the last person on earth whom one would try to disguise or camouflage in any way because he would be immediately identifiable. Nonetheless, he was an active member of the Republican movement and could be seen at checkpoints set up by the IRA ,wearing a mask covering his face. Any local person would have been easily able to identify him, and needless to say the police identified him, pulled him in and put pressure on him until he eventually must have told them something, because later he was taken away by his comrades and interrogated, sentenced to death and executed, his body discarded on a roadside in County Armagh.

In the meantime, all the other crazy incidents of parish life continued unabated. We had the strange occasion when the lady who came to church to go to confession one evening before Mass and, for one reason or another, fell asleep in the confession box and remained sleeping until long after the church was closed. When she awoke, she found herself alone, in complete silence and darkness, confined on all sides by wooden walls. Where, I wonder, did she think she was? There was the one-legged Scotsman who insisted on throwing his crutch like a javelin at my office window at two o'clock in the morning, and we had the fairly intoxicated couple who came seeking a lift to the lower end of town in the middle of the night and who presented the biggest problem when it came to getting them out of the car, for they had begun an argument and were so busily attacking one another that I had great difficulty in persuading them to vacate the car and let me get home to my bed. We had the incident of the policeman becoming isolated from his comrades and being rescued from undoubted danger by a very courageous priest. We had the death of two young men and the injury of a third when they tried to pursue an undercover intelligence soldier who retaliated with much superior fire-power.

These were just some of the incidents that occurred during my days in Long Tower. And, in the meantime, life had to go on as always, except that you were expected not merely to perform all your familiar parochial duties, but also to make allowances for the unfamiliar pattern of your parishioners' lifestyle by visiting them in Long Kesh and Magilligan and offering Mass for them. This was particularly strange during what was called the 'Dirty Protest', when prisoners refused to wear prison clothes and smeared their cells with excrement. No one accepted the fact that you might be completely stressed out from a night of disturbance as an excuse for not being there promptly in the morning to say Mass or whatever else might need to be done. It took its toll on all of us. I found it impossible not just to sleep but even to lie in bed, an affliction that still affects me. An hour or so after going to bed, my legs would begin to vibrate internally – I cannot find any other description for what was happening – until it became so bad that I had to rise and walk, initially around the house, but later around the parish, in an attempt to tire out my legs and allow me to get back to bed for a few hours sleep. I have no idea what the parishioners made of it, but on one occasion, I frightened the life out of a young man who was conducting some mysterious business at four o'clock in the morning when I suddenly rounded the corner and came upon him.

I started writing for radio while I was in Long Tower parish and eventually, I composed and delivered more than a hundred 'Thoughts for the Day', which I later published in book form, as well as numerous broadcasts for Radio 4 and the World Service.

The culture of Derry is very self-centred. The people firmly believe that they stand at the centre of the world, and that consequently the world is concerned with what happens to them. As an example, let me recall a visit I made to a senior Republican, who raised some contentious issues about the state of Magilligan Jail at the time. He expressed his dissatisfaction with the attitude of the bishop and the response of the local church, and eventually snapped at me, 'does the pope know about this?' I tried to imagine the pope asking someone to nip out and buy the *Derry Journal* and the *Londonderry Sentinel* so that he could find what was happening in Magilligan Jail. Earthquakes in Japan, tsunamis in the Philippines, civil war in Africa and so on would all have to be put on hold while the pope checked out the situation in Magilligan. I said, 'I wouldn't think so', to which he responded, 'Well, if he doesn't know, he should know.'

Nor is sensitivity always built into their conversation. A man asked my age shortly after I arrived in the Long Tower, when I was forty-two years old, and guessed it as fifty; when told that he was nearly ten years out, he congratulated me on being a fresh man for sixty. Even the younger generation can set you back on your heels. I foolishly boasted to a ten-year-old altar server that I could still fit into the cassock I had worn at my ordination twenty-five years earlier, and she asked, 'Why? Were you always fat?'

In spite of all the turmoil and the divisions within the city, I established very good relationships with the non-Catholic clergy in the town. It became a feature of our lives that I would entertain them to dinner on St Patrick's Day, and they in turn invited me to dine with them on many other occasions. The good relationship which we established then has endured to this very day, and we still meet when the opportunity arises. And, looking back, we find it hard to understand what the division was about, and certainly we find it hard to understand how it could have been in any way established as a religious division, because what joins us and what unites us is far greater than what supposedly separates us.

After seventeen and a half years in the Bogside I was transferred to Limavady. I had heard so many stories about the bigotry and the prejudice against the Catholic community that it was only when I spent some time in the parish that I realised that we had inherited an enormous amount of myth and legend. In fact, I found myself living in a parish where there was, first of all, an enormous amount of activity. Where else would you find a community that supported three churches, two parish halls, in which everything from bingo to charity shops was promoted: an ACE scheme that employed up to twenty men, a Silver Thread Club that catered for the elderly, but which was completely self sufficient, teams of men and women who organised everything from the St Vincent de Paul Society, the Legion of Mary, St Joseph's Young Priests' Society, religious education of the handicapped, saving schemes, Catholic Boy Scouts, Sunday collectors, readers, Pioneer Total Abstinence Association, as well as area representatives who kept us abreast of whoever was arriving or departing, not to mention a dedicated spiritual team who had persuaded even farmers' wives to adopt the lotus position and meditate for half an hour. Secondly, I quickly came to realise that the vast majority of people were utterly tired of conflict between Protestant and Catholic.

A little old lady told me that her granny used to take her to Portrush for holidays, and as they passed Limavady in the train her grandmother instructed her to close her eyes because they were passing by that terrible place called Limavady. That kind of attitude does not disappear overnight. Nonetheless, we tried to become involved in all kinds of different activities that could be shared by all the faiths. When we came to renovate St Mary's Church, so many people from so many different places of worship around the town were pleased to be invited to the reopening and had no hesitation whatever about sharing in it. I am sure my congregation in Limavady were bored out of their minds listening to me saying, 'You can only learn from people who are different from you'.

After fifteen years in Limavady, and fifty years in priesthood, I resigned. Whether I liked it or not, I was not energetic enough to deal with all the problems and all the responsibilities of parish life. Even before I arrived in Limavady, I had been suffering from angina and diabetes, but the miracle of modern medicine had kept me going for the ensuing years. I was able to renovate Christ the King Church for the Silver Jubilee and to do a major renovation on St Mary's that I still look back on with great pride.

I can honestly say that I found Limavady to be not just a great parish to work in but a wonderful community in which to live. The only ripple I experienced was more the fault of Louis, my Irish Terrier mongrel, than myself. He was more used to the carefree and undisciplined life around the streets of Derry than to the more orderly regime expected in Limavady. For instance, he frequently travelled from his home in Abercorn Road across to St Eugene's Cathedral where he refreshed himself with a drink from the holy water font before returning home. His misbehaviour in Limavady – whatever the nature of the crime – resulted in an anonymous letter, which not merely attacked his erratic ways, but which diverged into a tirade on the behaviour of the clergy, which the writer felt was exemplified by Fr Brendan Smith. I thought such an imaginative piece of correspondence deserved to be shared among a wider audience, so at Mass the following Sunday, I read it out in place of the sermon. I only wish my sermons could hold the attention of the congregation the way that letter did. That was the only anonymous letter I received in Limavady.

Spreading the Gospel of Christ is no easy task in today's world. Some clergy believe that this is best done by the solemn repetition of the words of Scripture from the pulpit every Sunday. Others, like myself, believe that if nobody is listening, it does not matter what you say, so my first priority is to make it interesting, and you can only do that by stealing wholesale the ideas and the stories of others, especially the stories. Good stories are hard to find, and good stories that you can use in a sermon are like gold dust.

I have used up all my good stories already, not merely in sermons but in books and broadcasting, so let me conclude with an example of a good story that you *cannot* use in a sermon.

A man goes to confession and confesses to having used awful language during the week. He feels terrible about it now.

'When did you use this awful language?', asks the priest.

'Well, I was playing golf, and I hit an incredible drive that looked like it would carry over 280 yards, but it hit a phone line that was stretched across the fairway and it fell just a hundred yards away'.

'Is that when you swore?', asks the priest.

'No, Father', says the man. 'After that, a squirrel ran out of the bushes and grabbed my ball in his mouth and began to run away with it'.

'Is THAT when you swore?', asks the priest again.

'Well, no. You see, as the squirrel was running away, an eagle swooped down out of the sky, grabbed the squirrel in his talons and began to fly away'.

'Is THAT when you swore?', asks the amazed priest.

'Not yet. You see, as the eagle carried the squirrel away, it flew over a bit of forest near the green and the squirrel dropped my ball into the forest'.

'Did you swear THEN?', asks the by-now impatient priest.

'No, because as the ball fell, it struck a tree, bounced through some bushes, careened off a big rock, rolled through a sand trap onto the green and stopped within six inches of the hole'.

There was a prolonged and pregnant silence in the confessional until the priest sighed deeply and said,

'Don't tell me you missed the f*****g putt?'

Broadcasts

Eduardo

The most touching lament for a child in the entire Scriptures is the lament of King David for his son Absalom, and yet Absalom was a spoilt brat, full of ambition and arrogance, with no concern for anyone but himself. However, when he died, David could not restrain his grief, and he went up to his bedroom and cried out loud. 'O my son, Absalom, my son, my son, Absalom! Would I had died instead of you, O Absalom, my son, my son'.

It is a dilemma that confronts every parent. They love their children, but sometimes their children can be such a disappointment. I sometimes try to restore the balance with this little story:

A hard-working couple return home and find a letter from their teenage daughter on the kitchen table. They open it and read:

'Dear Mummy and Daddy,

You have always taught me to be honest with you, so I do feel I should tell you about Eduardo, who was an assistant gardener here at school.

I have fallen deeply in love with Eduardo, who has initiated me into the joys of sex, and by the time you read this letter we shall be on the high seas back to Venezuela, which is Eduardo's homeland. Life has not been kind to Eduardo. If anything, he looks a little bit older than fifty-six, and apparently both his previous wives are absolutely awful, and do nothing but pester poor Eduardo for money to look after the children.

Of course, he doesn't have a bean, so to forget his troubles the poor man has to drink a lot. Don't you think that's sad? Eduardo and I will be setting up home in a tiny flat in what he calls the Soho of Caracas, and he has already got me a well-paid job in the little club downstairs, which I can go back to after I've had the baby.

Well, that's all for now. Will write again soon. All my love, Angie.

P.S. None of the above is true, but I failed my exams this morning, and I thought this might put things into perspective'.

The Other John Lennon

As told by a kindly neighbour

His name was John Lennon, but there the similarities ended. He had no possessions. Even the clothes on his back and the shoes on his feet did not belong to him. He had no money, no family, no friends that he knew of, and nowhere to shelter when the winter winds swept down from Mullaghash mountain, except the kitchen floor of a kindly neighbour, or more likely, the chilly expanse of an open barn or an empty hayshed.

I was visiting the home of my childhood, which was being renovated, and it brought back these vivid memories as I admired the skill with which the builder had incorporated the settle bed into the new bathroom. In my childhood, two or sometimes three of us slept in the settle bed, an ingenious alcove beside the hearth, almost like a berth on an ocean liner, with curtains drawn before it for privacy, but with a big enough opening left for us to observe what was going on in the earthen-floored kitchen.

Mostly, the comings and goings were predictable. Neighbours gathered in to catch up with the gossip, to discuss forthcoming fairs and prices, to smoke pipes and drink tea and spit into the fire before the time came to rise stiffly from the hard-backed chairs and head home to bed. Sometimes, however, it brought a glimpse of a foreign world into our kitchen – strangers from what seemed faraway places, miniature men with hunched backs and tiny legs, arms and fingers like a child, yet reaching out from a fully matured body. Sometimes fingers were missing, and sometimes the hands were so warped and bent that they could scarcely hold on to a cup of tea or a fork.

This was our introduction to John Lennon. One night, he suddenly appeared through the curtains before our hearth fire. Fascinated though we were, we had been taught only too well to say nothing when visitors called, much less to ask any personal questions, so we waited for the morning and then descended upon my mother with a litany of questions about the exotic stranger. Before she could begin, my father stepped in and solemnly set us down while he repeated his endlessly familiar dissertation on 'respect for people'. Not just handicapped people, but especially handicapped people. We must never comment on any personal feature, no matter how strange or alarming it might seem to us. His height, his legs, his arms, his head, his fingers – all these may seem strange to us, but to John they were the ordinary features of daily life, and woe betide any of us who made him feel otherwise. It was a lesson that had been taught relentlessly throughout our childhood, but this was clearly an unprecedented occasion for putting it into practice.

My father had met him on the road and they got into conversation. John gave some details of his extraordinary life. He was born with a huge array of physical handicaps and he never grew to more than four feet. He took to the roads as soon as he could escape from home, and survived by begging or by making artificial flowers from lengths of thin wire and coloured tissue paper which he sold around the houses either for money or in exchange for food. He slept where he could, and if he was lucky enough to be given shelter with a family, he slept on the floor, and in the morning took a cloth from his bag and a bar of soap and headed for the nearest water hole where he took his daily wash.

Inevitably, it finished up with my father offering him the hospitality of our home and the warmth of the kitchen floor. There was never any suggestion that my mother should be consulted before John was given the run of the house. Standard practice dictated that if my father thought someone deserved a place to stay, they were given a place to stay, and once John had established himself as a friend of the family, he became a regular caller. When he arrived he was seated before the hearth fire, wet clothes were hung up to dry, tea was made – or if John had gone hungry for a time, something more substantial – and I can still recall my mother gently pressing the slices of bread between John's two remaining fingers so that he could feed himself. A large mug, partially filled, made the tea easier to manage, and when bedtime came, the chairs were cleared back and a rug laid on the floor for John to sleep on.

My mother used to go around the house at bedtime with a bottle of holy water, sprinkling everyone and invoking God's blessing and protection on them, and as I lay dozing in my settle bed, I saw my mother gently and carefully sprinkling the holy water on John also, not so much in invocation, but rather it seemed, in thanksgiving for the privilege of being allowed to care for such a special child of God.

Technology

Technology, whether analogue or digital, has always separated the old from the young. Those of my generation can remember the videotape recorder and the problems we had with the timer. We were forever taping *Panorama* and the *Ten O'Clock News* instead of the entertaining rubbish that we wanted.

The digital revolution continues to outrun us, but such examples as the mobile phone are merely the tip of the iceberg. Instead, a new obstacle has swung across our path, creating an even greater chasm of misunderstanding between young and old, namely the English language.

It began with 'absolutely'. Where 'absolutely' came from, I have no idea, but suddenly it cut through all the laws and traditions of the English language and substituted a meaningless four-syllable word for the most precise and simple word in the language, 'Yes'. Nowadays, when asked if you would like a cup of tea you respond: 'Absolutely'.

From this starting point, young people have acquired the right to adopt and maintain a language that is entirely their own. Not merely have they adopted phrases from recent songs and films that are incomprehensible to their elders, they now employ words to which they have given a completely new meaning. For example, ask a child, 'how are you?', and instead of getting an account of their well-being you get an account of their behaviour. Instead of 'I'm well', they now say 'I'm good'. When you thank someone for services rendered they say, 'No problem', leading you to wonder, 'Was there a problem here that I missed?' When you suggest that they avoid the company of some unsuitable companion, they say, 'Right', when their tone implies a very definite 'Wrong'. In the local supermarket, when confronted by a veritable mountain of groceries, they will ask you if you have a 'wee' bag, and when you have exhausted yourself trying to convince your offspring that the path they are pursuing will lead to misery, their response is, 'Whatever'.

Sometimes I look back with nostalgia to the days when even grammar had its rules, before controversy became contro versy and no one dreamt of saying, 'it doesn't matter to you or I'.

Wouldn't it be wonderful if we could all go back to speaking the same language?

'Oh, absolutely!'

Too Good?

Is it possible, do you think, for a man to be too good to his neighbour? Certainly, it is possible for parents to be too good to their children. They will overlook their failings and encourage their selfishness in the belief that this is how a good parent should behave. The results of such an attitude can, of course, be catastrophic, especially when they are passed on to another generation. Even so, the best example I have encountered of this excessive dedication was a husband and wife combination – a truly generous husband and a cold and calculating wife.

After a life of unbounded generosity and limitless forgiveness, not merely to his wife but to everyone he encountered, the husband died and was welcomed with open arms into Heaven. God said: 'I have watched your unselfish generosity all down the years and as a reward I am willing to grant any request you ask'. The husband immediately pulled out a tattered old map of the Middle East from his pocket and said: 'All through my life, I have watched these nations fight against each other, despite all the efforts of peacemakers throughout the world to bring them together. They have brought death and destruction not merely to their enemies but to their friends and families. Only you can bring an end to this carnage'.

God took the map in his hands and perused it carefully, and with tears running down his cheeks, he addressed the husband. 'Not just for generations, but for centuries, these nations have fought one another. All efforts at reconciliation and a peaceful solution have failed. I have tried all methods of appeasement and compromise without success, and I greatly fear that it does not lie within my powers to grant this request. Is there possibly some other request that would be more feasible to grant?'

The husband thought for a moment and said: 'Well, when we were on earth together, my wife and I used to take occasional weekend breaks together, but it seemed that no matter how carefully we planned or where we chose to go, my wife always ran into difficulties. Either the food was not good or the staff were unfriendly or the climate was harsh. Nothing seemed to make my wife happy. And I am wondering, could you give her a weekend in Heaven, because there is no way that she could find any fault with what you would provide?'

God looked steadily at the husband for a considerable time, and eventually he spoke: 'Here, let me have another look at that map'.

Photography

Back in the early days of my ministry, nearly half a century ago, I was a junior curate in a country parish where life was never too hectic, and where I was left free to pursue my long-standing interest in photography. I lived in a large rambling house, with a windowless alcove under the stairs which served as an ideal darkroom, and where a vast sitting room provided ample exhibition space in those pre-digital days. I could not afford to frame the prints so I simply stuck, or even nailed, them to the walls until there was not an inch of space that was not adorned with a photograph.

And then came word that the bishop was coming, and remember, in those days, everyone was afraid of the bishop. He was going to rededicate the church that I had just renovated and confirm the local candidates, and my sitting room was chosen as his operational headquarters for the day. You can see my dilemma. Do I strip the walls of all traces of photography and present to the bishop a newly painted image of tasteful normality, or take a chance of being branded forever as the first graffiti artist in the locality? I decided to chance it and left everything in place. The bishop duly arrived and had tea surrounded by the photographs, but made absolutely no comment. We talked of this and that, and at the appointed time, he rededicated the church and returned to the house for more tea. Again, no comment. He then went back to the church and confirmed the children, and returned to the sitting room when he had finished. Again, no comment. When it came time to go home, he gathered up his belongings, looked briefly around the room and said, 'Mmm … Interested in photography?', and departed.

Today everyone is a photographer, but no one preserves photographs. Yesterday's photographer was a man of power and influence. He made an appointment for you to visit his studio with its massive lights, his wooden tripod and his huge glass plate camera. He, and he alone, decided what image of you would be passed down the ages, and if it did not measure up to your expectations, too bad. Let me finish by quoting one of these superior beings when he was confronted by a woman who complained that the photograph he had taken of her did not do her justice. Without hesitation or apology he replied, 'Missus, its mercy you need and not justice!'

Men and Women

If the only thing we sought from the Lord was a higher place at the banquet table in the Kingdom of Heaven, He would not be too displeased with us, but instead we go looking for all kinds of gifts and gadgets because we think these things will make our life on earth happier. Sadly, it does not work out that way. We ask for gifts without ever considering their real value or usefulness to us. Let me set the background for this story.

Most married men will freely admit that even after years of domestic life, they have no understanding of the impulses that dictate the choice of such simple things as fabric and furnishings in the home. Even the most basic items – such as cushions and curtains – remain a complete mystery. For a man, a cushion serves a distinct and fundamental purpose, to make the seat that you are sitting on as comfortable as possible. Everything else is subsidiary. Similarly, the purpose of a curtain is to keep the neighbours from looking into your private apartment. Colour, fabric, pattern, weight, design, are all peripheral. Little wonder, then, that when it comes to exotic attachments such as valances or tie-backs or duvet covers, there is a complete breakdown of communication on the domestic front.

Men are not geared to cope with the complexities of family life, and in an effort to justify themselves, they have come up with a simple explanation for this breakdown: 'women have the whole day at home with nothing to do'. Even though some women have upset the whole argument by going out to work, those who remain at home are inevitably left with the time to create decorative and ornamental items for the home that are not seen as essential – or even useful – by their husbands, and merely entrench them in their belief that the phrase 'going out to work' is in direct contrast and contradiction to the phrase 'staying at home'. Husbands go out to work. Wives stay at home. This was a basic, if not misguided principle of domestic life until, that is, one foolish husband tried to change the situation.

Convinced that he was slaving away at work while his wife was putting her feet up at home, he implored the Almighty to allow him to change places with her, and God in his wisdom granted his request. He awoke next day as a woman. So he got up, cooked breakfast, woke the children, set out their school clothes, fed them their breakfast, packed their lunches, drove them to school, came home and picked up the dry cleaning, took it to the cleaners, shopped for groceries, took them home and balanced the family finances, cleaned out the cat's litter tray and washed the dog.

He took a cup of tea, then made the beds, did the laundry, vacuumed and dusted the living room, swept and mopped the kitchen floor, ran to the school to pick up the children, listened to them squabbling on the way home, organised them to do their homework and then did all the ironing.

At five o'clock he began peeling potatoes and washing and chopping vegetables for the dinner. He then cooked and served dinner and afterwards tidied up the kitchen, loaded the dishwasher, bathed the children, read them a story and put them to bed. By half ten he was exhausted, and even though there was still work to be done, he went to bed, where he was expected to make love with a certain degree of enthusiasm.

When he woke up the next morning, completely exhausted, he fell on his knees and implored God: 'I was so wrong, God. I should never have envied my wife for staying at home. Please, let's change back to what we were'. God, in his infinite wisdom, replied: 'My son, I think you have learned your lesson, and I will be happy to change you back. But you'll have to wait nine months. You see, you got pregnant last night, with twins'.

Be very careful about what you ask from God. Your prayers may be answered!

Doggie Comfort

Medical experts have recently told us that by simply cuddling up to a pet dog, you can lower your heart rate by up to forty per cent. I thought everybody knew this already, though I couldn't have put a figure on it, but just in case the medical experts may believe that they have covered every ramification in this matter, I would like to propose a further contribution to this debate. The larger and hairier the dog, the more effective its soothing power!

I mention this because I have a large German shepherd, the size of a young donkey, who likes nothing better than to lick your face and generally welcome you into the family circle, but inevitably he creates reservations in the minds of a lot of people about his motives, so they tend to keep a healthy distance between him and their loved ones. Young mothers stiffen perceptively when he appears, and put a protective arm around the shoulders of their offspring, who in turn also stiffen up, creating an atmosphere of stress and tension which the dog inevitably interprets as aggression. And so, another child grows up deprived of the comfort and the companionship of the animal world, unaware that when God created all these things, he didn't do it to terrorise us, but because he found them all to be very good. Here is a little story:

A man wanted to take his dog on holiday with him so he wrote to the hotel owner asking if his dog might stay in the room with him at night. He was, he assured the owner, a clean and well-groomed animal and very well behaved.

The owner of the hotel wrote back:

'I have been operating this hotel for twenty years, and in all that time, I have never had a dog steal towels or bedclothes, or silverware from the dining room, or pictures off the walls. I have never had to evict a dog in the middle of the night for getting drunk and disorderly, nor have I ever had a dog leave without paying his bill.

Your dog will be most welcome at my hotel. And if your dog will vouch for you, you will be welcome to stay here too'.

Birthday Party

I caught sight of a four-year-old's birthday party recently. It was not being held in the front room at home, as you might expect. A large private room in a local hotel had been hired to accommodate about thirty juvenile guests, and as they descended from their motorised transport, each was presented with a pictorial menu and asked to make a choice. The main birthday present was a multi-coloured bicycle with stabilisers and enough gears to qualify for the Tour de France, not to mention the accessories – the helmet, the jacket, the kneepads, the reinforced gloves, and the goggles. Before they departed, the guests were presented with a glitzy bag of goodies to sustain them on the journey home.

I couldn't help but wonder, 'Have I lost the plot completely? Am I living in a real world or has it passed me by? Imagine! Your own bicycle at four years of age! Adults had bicycles in my day, but only the kind-hearted and the careless let you set foot on them, and even then you had to share, a passenger on the carrier and another on the crossbar. If you fell off, as you inevitably did, you suffered your wounds in silence. If your injuries could not be concealed, you submitted to treatment with Dettol and hot water, or, if Dettol was not available, with a dab of Jeyes Fluid left over from the sheep dipping. You walked a mile and a half to and from school in all weathers. You got slapped for getting sums or spellings wrong, and if you were foolish enough to report your punishment, you were slapped when you got home. You worked at all kind of chores, from sweeping yards to cutting thistles, from driving cows to pumping water, and if you missed out on any of these essential duties, you got a sharp bleech around the back of the legs with a sally rod. You said private prayers every morning and family prayers every evening. You confessed your sins on Saturday night and attended church on Sunday morning'.

At the end of the day, the question has to be asked, 'how did we survive it all?' If the suffocating attention given to today's generation is really necessary, will they be better people? Will they live far longer and create a better world? Will there be some return for the sacrifices their parents are making for them?

There are eight members in my family. The youngest is seventy-three and the oldest eighty-five. The youngest still runs half marathons, but we all have our own way of going mad. We must have got something right.

Husband Supermarket

Any attempt at humour must contain an element of truth. There is nothing funny about calling a thin man 'Fatty'. You are merely being abusive and boring. Of course, it does not follow that if your statement contains an element of truth, it must be humorous. The Scriptures are full of profound truths, but there is not a great deal of humour to be found in them. About the only laugh we get is from Sarah, the wife of Abraham, when she was told that she was going to have a baby at ninety, which, reasonably enough, she thought was hilarious.

I reached this conclusion about humour when reading a story about a supermarket that specialised in selling husbands. As you might guess, the story was not meant to be taken too seriously. The supermarket consisted of five floors with the quality of available husbands improving with each floor.

The first floor was a sort of bargain basement. The sign outside said, 'these men have jobs and love children'. It drew a few takers, but not much enthusiasm.

The second floor said, 'these men have high-paying jobs. They love children and are extremely good-looking'. As one might imagine, this floor had more takers, but some women still insisted on going to floor three.

The sign there said, 'these men have high-paying jobs, are extremely good-looking, love children, and help with the housework'. It is hard to see how you could improve on this. Even so, there were some who insisted on continuing up to the fourth floor.

The sign there said, 'these men have high-paying jobs, love children, are extremely good-looking, help with the housework and have a strong romantic streak'.

Nobody could figure out how you were going to improve on this. Nonetheless, a few women continued up to the fifth floor where the sign said, 'this floor is empty, and exists only to prove that God himself could not please some women'.

As I said in the beginning, any attempt at humour must contain some element of truth.

Driving Livestock

As I grow older, I find myself doing all the little jobs around the house that I used to hate doing as a child – sweeping the yard, tidying the shed, cutting hedges, gathering litter – though, thank God, it is now a matter of choice. If I feel tired, or even lazy, I come inside for a quick snooze. There was always work to be done around our house, and there were two types of work that I hated – cutting thistles and driving livestock. At ten years of age, I was handed a scythe – a heavy, man-sized and usually blunt instrument – and pointed towards a ten-acre field of thistles. It was tiring, boring and, above all, lonely work. However, it was at least seasonal work only, whereas driving cattle was permanent hard labour. The cattle ambled along the road at their own pace, stopping on the verges for a quick snack, before being chivvied on again, or making a quick dash for freedom into any open gateway they encountered. You had to hustle what was left of the herd past the gateway, then run into the field and round up the strays, and somehow persuade them to follow the rest of the herd rather than making a break for home. Fortunately, traffic was light in those days. More than two cars per mile was a bad day.

However, the most embarrassing drive I ever had to carry out was a large sow that had to be escorted on foot for a conjugal visit to the boar on the other side of Omagh. Needless to say every passer-by had good advice to offer: 'Get up on her back, son, and give yourself a rest'. Or, 'what breed of dog is that you have, son?' But for sheer unpredictability and stupidity, nothing can compare with sheep. On one occasion, I had to drive a flock of them through the town of Omagh, and at every opportunity they broke loose and stampeded through gardens and flower beds, and where one lunatic went the others followed. The only occasion when they failed to follow this rule, thank God, was when I was driving them up Castle Street and suddenly heard a piercing shriek from an upstairs window. Like everyone else, I stopped to see who was being murdered, and quickly learned that one of my sheep had bolted through an open doorway, straight up the stairs, and into the nearest bedroom. I suppose it was the kind of thing that would take anyone by surprise.

I have a sympathetic attitude to all of God's creatures, but I must admit there are times when I wonder why the Almighty should place such dim and erratic animals as sheep on his right hand and such independent and resourceful animals as goats on his left.

Silence

'Let each of them keep silence in church, and speak to himself and to God'. That is St Paul, writing to the Corinthians. 'There was silence in Heaven for about half an hour'. That is St John writing in the last book of the Bible, Revelation.

Well, I suppose half an hour wasn't bad. When it comes to learning to keep silence in sacred places, the human race is still in playschool. Even in Heaven, I'm sure there was one chatterbox who couldn't keep quiet for more than half an hour.

Even without the benefit of divine intervention, the world knows the importance of silence. 'Silence is golden', we are told. 'Silent Night, Holy Night'. You don't expect to hear someone singing 'Noisy Night, Holy Night'. But for some unfathomable reason, the human race cannot resist the temptation to sabotage every attempt to create a zone of silence, from the very depths of the forests to the very house of God himself.

In days gone by, public building were havens of peace. The silence was so pervasive that one was tempted to whisper, even in the washrooms. We might have been taught from old that God is found in the quiet breeze rather than in the earthquakes and the tornadoes, but we still continue to make noise.

The ancient monks used to take a single word and meditate on it for days rather than hours, until they became completely absorbed in God, before necessity compelled them to return to the world of cleaning cells and preparing meals.

The practice of meditating spilled over into the parish churches, and novices in the practice sat quietly before God, waiting for Mass or service to begin, unaware that they were following in the steps of the great mystics and saints of the past. They were content just to be, and to be with God.

And then came the saboteurs, the noisy exhibitionists, with their pious novenas and their papal approval, and ruined everything. Can anyone think of a way of bringing back silence, not just to churches, but everywhere. Imagine what a blessing it would be!

29 December

I knew 29 December was special somehow, but I could not remember why, and then it came back to me. My brother's birthday. He should be eighty-three this morning. He is a priest also. He studied for the English-speaking missions and finished up in New Zealand.

It was a big step back in 1957, and the powers-that-be did not make it any easier. I was not allowed to attend his ordination at All Hallows in Dublin because I was studying for the priesthood in Rome, but I was assured that he would get home for a holiday after ten years and I could see him then!

I went out to visit him in 1974 and experienced the All Hallows culture at first hand. Graduates of the college are to be found all over the world, so when they travel, they stay with one another. During my time in New Zealand, we toured the entire country and never once had we to stay in a hotel, though even we were surprised by our experience in the South Island. As we came up the East Coast, we headed as usual for the nearest presbytery, but found no one at home. However, the house was open so we sat ourselves down and waited for the pastor to return. Several hours passed and no one appeared, so we boiled the kettle and made ourselves a cup of tea. Several more hours passed and night fell, and still no one appeared, so we explored the house and found a spare room with an empty bed, which we duly furnished with coverings from the hot press, and went to bed.

Next morning we rose and went to the adjoining church where everything was just as wide open and accessible. We said Mass together, came back to the house and made breakfast, and before leaving left a note thanking the absent incumbent for his hospitality. We topped up at the local filling station before leaving, and, in passing, asked the owner was Father so-and-so not being a little careless, leaving the house and church wide open to any passing burglar?

'When you leave this town', he said, 'you have to go a hundred miles north or a hundred miles south before you can cut off to go anywhere else; and apart from that, nobody locks doors about here, and a stranger would stand out like a sore thumb'.

That's how it used to be at home, I thought.

I wonder if it is still the same out there.

Past

The Ulster poet Maurice James Craig wrote a poem about the land of his birth which contains the immortal lines:

'It's to hell with the future, we'll live in the past.
May the Lord in His mercy be kind to Belfast'.

And we all live in the past, up to our ears, and we are unlikely to escape it unless we admit our unwillingness to change in a changing world and to put the past behind us.

We commemorate battles from hundreds of years ago, rebellions and revolutions, wars and uprisings, and the most notable feature, common to all of them, is that people have suffered and died in them. We have some kind of obsession with failure. I often wonder, for instance, what do strangers make of our celebration, not to say obsession, with the *Titanic*? Imagine a stranger from Tierra del Fuego, who has never heard of it, visiting Belfast for the first time.

'This was a mighty big ship. What kind of records did it set?'

'It sank on its maiden voyage'.

We need to forget the past and start looking at the blessings God has given us. Even the weather is in our favour. Experience has taught us that the past is a very unreliable place. We think, because it is old, it is trustworthy. We should know better. For instance, most of us have had at least some experience of the Troubles. How much of what is written today truthfully reflects that experience? Have the sinners all really turned into saints? Was no one to blame for the chaos and the turmoil we had to endure for thirty years?

Let me finish with an example of our obsession with the past and the craziness it can lead to. The grandfather of a clerical colleague emigrated to America in the early 1900s and fell in with a Danish gentleman making the same journey. For several days their friendship flourished, but one day, without warning, the Irishman physically attacked the unfortunate Dane. When asked for a reason for this unprovoked attack the Irishman said, 'You are one of the so-and-sos who killed Brian Boru'.

'But that was a thousand years ago', said the Dane.

'That may be', replied the Irishman. 'But I only heard about it last night!'

Mental vs. Manual

The big problem about reading books in our house when I was young was finding somewhere to do it without interruption. You could not sit down in the kitchen and pull out a book, for my father would have immediately pointed to you in a very emphatic manner and said, 'have you nothing better to be doing at this time of day than reading books? Come you with me and I'll find you something useful to do'. This was the standard reaction, no matter what time of day it was. The only way you could escape interruption was by locking yourself in the toilet, but that did not always please the other domestic clients who were patiently waiting to put the facilities to a more orthodox use.

And that was how it was until I progressed to full-time education. I do not mean going to school every day and doing homework – that, after all, was just another kind of donkey work – but sitting at a desk for hours on end trying to dissect and analyse terms like 'the philosophy of being' or 'the mathematical concept of time'. That was real intellectual work, and most people who are confronted with it will opt for a simple job like shovelling sand or pushing a wheelbarrow. In fact, most people will go to great lengths to create this kind of work rather than sit down and study.

In my student days, the young man in the room next to me could never be persuaded to sit down at his desk and get stuck into the books when recreation ended. Instead, he was liable to start spring cleaning. You could hear him moving furniture and sweeping floors and rearranging bookshelves, and generally messing about until the end of study was in sight, and then he would open a few books and leave them on display for the elevation and admiration of any passer-by.

I can remember the likes of farm labourers greeting us on our way home from school with pearls of wisdom like, 'Ah, education is a great thing. Sure it's easy carried'. Well, let me pass my own judgement on this intellectual nugget.

Scholarly investigation and literary composition are infinitely more exhausting than manual labour, and they do not get any easier with age. When you are eighty years old and you sit down to compose another 'Thought for the Day', you bring out the laptop – or in my case the jotter – and gaze intently at it, and search furiously through your mind and memory for some intriguing subject, and find nothing, so you get up and start spring cleaning, and only when you are faced with an absolute deadline will you produce anything on paper; but, be not downhearted. You will have the cleanest house in the country.

Fashion

As I walked down Market Street in Limavady recently, a lady complimented me on how well dressed I was. Twenty yards further on another lady made the same comment, and a little later a man expressed his surprise that I looked so smart. In all, before I got to the end of the street, five people had remarked on how well dressed I was!

Never before, in my entire seventy-eight years, had anyone complimented me on my appearance. In fact, the only occasion I can remember when my outfit was mentioned is one I would prefer to forget. In the Spartan post-war years, my mother had my father's square-shouldered honeymoon coat adjusted to fit me, and sent me out into the streets of Omagh looking like a cross between a Sephardic Jew and a Chicago gangster. The lack of comment since then is understandable if you remember that from the day I started to study for the priesthood, I had to wear a black suit at all times. If I appeared in public at all, I wore a black suit.

In one way it was very convenient, but it was utterly boring. Essentially, it made you invisible. For fifty-seven years I dressed in black, and even when I retired four years ago, I made no attempt to dress fashionably. And then a good friend bought me a smartly cut jacket for my birthday last year, and I realised I could not go about with the rest of the outfit laughing at it, so I bought a shirt in Asda, a tie in Poundland, a pair of trousers on the internet and a pair of soft shoes for my diabetic feet.

Somehow it all seemed to come together, and I ceased to be the invisible man. I still wear my black suit for all formal and religious occasions, but I wear my new outfit when I can, and the results are most gratifying.

I can offer no explanation for it, not even the one offered by the Dungiven man who was known for his laid-back dress sense. When complimented by a mischievous acquaintance at a wedding on his latest attire – a Fair-Isle pullover and grey flannels – he answered, 'When you're young and good-looking, you're easy dressed'.

Trademarks

When I was growing up, you were never encouraged to develop your talents or display your abilities. It was assumed that if you had any gifts or talents, others would notice them and ask you to display them. I later discovered that many of my generation had the same experience. Modesty was the cornerstone of our upbringing. It may have seemed virtuous to parents and other mentors, but in fact it was destructive of the confidence and security that we all need to cope with life. I was already well into my forties when a friend suggested that I write something for radio – for better or for worse, I haven't stopped since.

Modern businesses have no hesitation about standing before the world and declaring, 'I manufacture a worthwhile product. I am proud to put my name on this article, for all the world to see, because it is a sound product'. In the past, it was Du Pont and Amtrac and Shell Oil and Ford and Chrysler and Stelco. Now it is Apple and Microsoft and Google and Facebook and Twitter.

Today we may have gone to the other extreme, and children are now encouraged, it may be said, to display even mediocre talents, in the hope of boosting their confidence and outshining their rivals. It doesn't always achieve its purpose, and even when it does, it can be a two-edged sword.

Perhaps it can best be explained by the experience of a County Derry blacksmith, who for many years carried on a modest but adequate business, until one day he was visited by a travelling American who pointed out to him that in his country, every successful manufacturer had his own insignia, his own trademark that identified his work to the world. So the blacksmith crafted himself a trademark, which he impressed on every horseshoe and five-barred gate from that onwards. Until, that is, a critical neighbour was heard to remark, 'Not a bit need had he for a trademark. You would know his rotten oul' work anywhere'.

The Prodigal Son

A man had two sons with him in the family grocery business. The younger son came to him one day and said, 'Listen, Pop, this cabbage and cornflakes business is a real bore. The whole scene bugs me. I gotta get out of here and live a little before I'm a real old man. Like, I'll be twenty-one in another month. You and squarehead can have the business between you. I'll just take whatever bread is coming to me, and split'. His father tried to talk him out of the idea, but his friends told him he would be crazy to miss the chance to see a bit of life. After all, you're only young once.

A few days later, he took off for London and set about having a good time. He met many other young men like himself and they lived a swinging life. He got himself a nice little flat – outrageously expensive – but all his new friends came to visit him, night and day. They told him where to buy the best booze and even taught him how to smoke pot. They also introduced him to liberated young women, who also wanted to live a little, and between them, they explored the nightspots of the city and the exotic entertainments that were unheard of at home.

Eventually, of course, his money ran out – and so too did his friends. He tried to borrow from the closest of them, but they slipped quietly away and gave him nothing. He got a job working in a rather seedy hotel kitchen, sweeping floors and emptying the slops, but his health gave out and he got the sack. He had no money and nowhere to sleep, so he went to a hostel for the homeless. A repulsive old man kept making passes at him so he left and tried sleeping rough in a derelict factory nearby. Every day he grew thinner and paler, until finally he decided to end it all by jumping into the river.

Fortunately, a kind old man was passing by at the time, and he spoke to him and persuaded him to go home to his parents, as a last resort.

His mother did not know him when he walked in the door, and she started crying when he spoke to her. His father said, 'You must be tired, son. Have a bath and something to eat and we'll talk later'. The young man could not think of anything to say. He just sat there and cried his heart out. 'It's all right son', his father said, 'we all have to learn, and most of us only learn by experience'.

And that is where we usually finish with the prodigal son. But in doing so, we completely overlook the other prodigal son in the Scriptures – Jesus, the son of Joseph and Mary. He came from a very upright and religious family. They all went up to Jerusalem to visit the Temple and to worship God, but when he was about twelve years of age, Jesus just left his parents and wandered off on his own. It took a week of frantic searching, and we are told that his parents were overcome when they found him. His mother said to him bluntly and angrily, 'My child, why have you done this to us? See how worried your father and I have been looking for you'. In the best teenage tradition, Jesus tried to justify himself. 'Did you not know that I must be about my father's business?'

We do not know what response Mary made to this remark, but whatever she said, it was direct and to the point, for in the next sentence we are told that Jesus went down with them and came to Nazareth and lived under their authority.

And the effects of this tough line by his parents? Jesus increased in wisdom and stature and in favour with God and men.

Maybe that is how to rear children.

The Work of Worship

Any broadcaster will tell you that you have to be careful about what you say on radio. Too many people are listening, and some of them may even remember what you have said. But an experienced broadcaster will tell you that you have to be far more careful about what you do not say. Too many people are not listening and they may remember something completely different from what you said.

For example, in a broadcast a few months ago, I mentioned lawyers and even told a joke about them. Shortly afterwards, I had a phone call from a lady whose daughter was a lawyer, challenging me for having said, or so her friend who had been listening had told her, that lawyers were the biggest villains on earth. Now, tempting as it may be to make sweeping statements about any body of people who charge so much for their services, it gave little credit to my intelligence, or that of the producer, to suggest that I would make such an unwarranted and such an obviously false statement.

What I actually said about lawyers was that I have invariably found them to be a pleasant if serious body of people – a comment I would be more than happy to apply to the clergy – but somehow or other, this lady's friend heard me describe them as villains. So we have to be careful about what we do not say.

Listeners tend to respond to what I might call certain trigger words. If, for example, I mention Daniel O'Donnell, they assume that I am talking about country and western music, when in fact I may be discussing the price of houses in County Kildare. If I mention Sinéad O'Connor, the assumption is that I am discussing shaven heads or feminist issues, when in fact I may be talking about her singing ability. My point is, you have to listen if you want to know what is going on. You have to pay attention. And that involves a certain amount of work. And if you don't listen, you will come away with all kinds of rare ideas about what has been said. And this is just as true in the world of worship as it is in the world of entertainment. You will find people coming out of church without any idea of what has been said because they have not listened. They have forgotten that worship is hard work.

This is Holy Week, the most concentrated week of worship in the whole year. Unless you are willing to listen, unless you are willing to work at your worship, this is going to be one very long, boring week.

Our Lost Children

We are told that God sent His Son into the world so that it might be saved through Him. What we are not told is why God loved the world so much. After all, the people of this world had very little time or respect for God or His Son. They disregarded His teaching and they treated His Son with violence and contempt. But God still continued to love them. Why? Well, we can never know the mind of God. We can only learn from human experience, and based on that experience we know that the most profound and tender relationship is that of parent and child, and particularly that of mother and child.

If I may digress for a moment, many years ago a good Irish Catholic mother was asked which she would choose first, her son or her husband, and she replied indignantly, 'You would hardly expect me to pass over my own flesh and blood for some strange man'. If that is true, we can only conclude that the most compelling reason why God should love us is that he created us, and for that same reason a father and mother who have brought a child into the world, who have, in short, created it, experience a closeness and an affection that surpasses all other human relationships.

When the Son of God rose from the dead, His purpose was to convince His friends and His followers that there is a new life beyond the grave; not the old life of this earth but a life that is free of all the limitations of the earth, and yet a life that reflects our life on earth. Just as Jesus spoke to his friends and followers after death, we too will speak to our children after death, whether they die before us or after us, whether they die before birth or after birth. We will be united with them in this new life for all eternity, for even the gift of eternal life without our children and our friends would be nothing more than solitary confinement. The joy of this world comes from our friendship with others, and the joy of the next world comes only with our reunion with all those who were close to us on earth. We waited patiently for them to join us at birth in this world, and nursed our grief when they could not join us. They now wait expectantly for us to rejoin them in their world.

May I finish with a prayer by the Victorian poet Christina Rossetti:

'Give, I pray Thee, to all children, grace reverently to love their parents, and lovingly to obey them. Teach us all that filial duty never ends or lessens; and bless all parents in their children and all children in their parents. O Thou in whom the fatherless find mercy, make all orphans, I beseech Thee, loving and dutiful unto thee, their true Father. Be Thy will their law, Thy house their home, Thy love their inheritance. And I earnestly pray Thee, comfort those who have lost their children, giving mothers grace to be comforted though their children are no more; and grant us all faith to yield our dearest treasures unto Thee with joy and thanksgiving, that where with Thee our treasure is, there our hearts may be also. Thus may we look for and hasten unto the day of union with Thee, and re-union with our children. Amen.'

The Magi

All is quiet in Bethlehem. The census is over. The people have gone home. The young couple are still sheltering in the stable, but now they have the child to care for. The innkeeper has taken pity on them on account of the baby and has allowed them to remain there. They are, apparently, a poor young couple without any friends. Their only visitors are a few rather smelly shepherds who came down the hill on the night of the birth, but they have not been back again. It is obvious that this couple is not used to being away from home. There is a shyness about them, a willingness to accept whatever is happening, all the time trusting that everything will turn out well, even when there is no evidence to support it.

One day, however, everything changes. The village is suddenly stirred into action. Visitors have arrived – and visitors such as the village has never seen before. These are not just rich men, but men from a different country, who wear their wealth as though it were their everyday clothes. They have come from Herod's court, they say, and they want to see the child. At the mention of Herod, a chill silence descends on the villagers. No one wants to talk about Herod's business. It can be dangerous. Eventually, however, someone directs the travellers to the only newborn child they know of – the one in the stable.

There is no trouble. There are no arrests. They come, they leave fabulous gifts, and then they go away; and suddenly the young people are different people. They have rich friends, so now they are moved out of the stable and given the best room the inn can offer, but not for long. The rich men depart, and then the young couple depart, and right on the heels of their departure come Herod's soldiers, killing and slaughtering all the babies under two years of age. There is turmoil and confusion in the village, but one thing is certain. It had something to do with the young couple and the baby. Maybe they should have treated them better. Maybe they were important people in disguise. They must have been. They had friends in high places, friends who could reach into the heart of Herod's court and learn his intentions and give the young couple time to escape the massacre.

The soldiers and the census takers and the travellers have finally left, but the question remains. Who were these people? Who was this child they came to visit?

Church Unity

Church unity in Northern Ireland is not the simple commodity you find in other parts of the world. Here it inevitably involves political unity also, and that makes it an almost impossible dream.

When it comes to godly things, we have to widen our horizons and speak in very broad and flowing terms. When it comes to the world in which we live, we have to be crisp and precise, for failure to do so can be quite catastrophic. If a pilot travelling from one end of the world to the other punches the wrong directions into his compass – even by a tenth of a degree – he may, indeed he probably will, finish up in the ocean, and if I disregard the word 'not' in a notice that says, 'High voltage. Do not touch', I may finish up in a body bag.

When dealing with godly things, as I say, we need to be broad-minded and even vague, for the tiny glimpse that we get of God through prayer and study – even on a good day – has to be fitted into the vast pattern that is God himself, and it may be that the lines and angles of our picture of God may not fit the pattern of God's picture – and it may not fit by a lot more than point one of a degree – so I should hesitate about trying to impose my patterns and perceptions of God on my neighbour, because he may be approaching God from a completely different angle. Like two men approaching a horse, one from the front and one from the rear, they will look a bit ridiculous if they both maintain that their viewpoint is the only true one.

Where God is concerned, we need to be able to admit that maybe we don't know. We may not be able to answer with the same abrasiveness as my friend Sammy, a good Presbyterian from Larne, long since gone to his maker, but we can only admire his spirit. He was asked by a mischievous Catholic if he believed in Purgatory. Sammy did not believe in Purgatory, but he did not want to get into a fight over it, so he pondered the matter for a moment and then he answered. 'I don't know about Purgatory, but I hope there's a hell, for there's a few boys around here I would like to see in it'.

A Tent of Clay

Have you ever noticed how difficult it is to think carefully about anything if your body is not feeling well? If you have a roaring toothache, there is no way you want to get caught up in a deep discussion about the political situation in Outer Mongolia. I find it very hard to pray if I even have a headache, and prayer doesn't call for any mental gymnastics. Somehow, any additional burden, whether it is physical pain or mental anxiety or concern about possessions, makes the body feel solid and heavy and keeps the mind from working effectively. The Book of Wisdom has a wonderful phrase for it. 'This tent of clay weighs down the teeming mind'. Can you imagine anything more awful than a tent of clay? It reminds me of wet potato fields with the mud sticking like heavy glue to your boots and the tails of your coat. Little wonder, then, that today's readings should warn us not to carry any unnecessary burdens on the journey through life. Every extra pound slows us down. We do need a certain amount of necessary baggage. If you are going to climb a mountain, you have to prepare both for the fine weather in the foothills, the bracing weather on the slopes and the freezing weather on the summit. But you are going to take a long look at a man who tackles it with a crate of beer under his arm or a set of golf clubs on his back.

To make speed towards Heaven, we have to unload all the useless baggage. In today's second reading, Paul writes a very discreet and tender little letter to his friend Philemon, and suggests that it would be a good thing for him to unload a certain burden, or rather, not to try to pick it up again, for the remainder of his life.

This is an unusual burden. Not a piece of property, nor an item of wealth, but a human being, his runaway slave Onesimus. Paul suggests that especially since Onesimus has now come to believe, like them, in the saving power of Jesus Christ, it will make Philemon happier if he forgets about the slave that he once owned and welcomes this man back as a brother. It will undoubtedly cost him money, the price of a slave, but it will make him a better and therefore a happier man, and he will earn Paul's undying gratitude. It seems a rather reasonable request. However, when Christ comes to talk about these things, he is neither discreet, nor tender, nor even reasonable. He says, 'If any man comes to me without hating his father, mother, wife, children, brothers and sisters, he cannot be my disciple'. It is what by any standards would be described as a tall order. He wants us not just to unload the excess baggage, but to dump the most essential and important people in our lives. And, believe it or not, the idea is not new. Way back in the early part of the Bible, in the Book of Deuteronomy, Moses describes the Levite, the holy man, as one who says, 'I do not regard my father, my brother I do not acknowledge, and I refuse to recognise my own children'.

Now, we obviously have to understand statements like these properly, for there is no sense in telling us to honour our father and mother one day, and another day telling us to hate them. Back in those days, people tended to be much less precise and accurate in their speech. They were more concerned with moving the imagination rather than the brain. After all, very few of them would have had any education at all. So they painted pictures and told vivid stories and even exaggerated a little in order to make their point.

Keeping this in mind, then, the message of Christ in this instance is loud and clear. You must not put anything – possessions, politics or people – before me. If there is a clash of interests, Christ must come first. And remember that we are never attracted to evil by itself. It is only when evil looks good or wise or effective that we follow it. Cheating a little at work or business to provide more money for your wife and children. Turning someone down for a job or promotion because your wife doesn't like them. Blackening a troublemaker's character or killing a political enemy. There is an attractive side to all of these evil deeds. And resisting that attraction is only part of being loyal to Christ, of being a disciple. There is also a lot of pain and effort and downright persecution as well. A narrow road, a small gate, nowhere to lay his head, no looking back, only insults, rejection, hatred and persecution even unto death. That's what a disciple can expect.

Only a fool will not hesitate before taking on such a life. Like the builder or the warrior king, he sits down and considers whether he can handle such a task with the talents and the equipment available to him. Unlike the builder and the warrior, he doesn't try to increase his supplies. Given enough money or enough soldiers, any builder or warrior could complete the task. The disciple works in the opposite direction. He gets rid of as much equipment as possible. He only keeps what is useful or necessary for the job. That is why Christ is so fond of the poor. They have no excess baggage to hold them back, for sometimes they are deprived of even the necessities, and that is why those with plenty must be ready to share. Of course, it is not always easy to determine what is necessary. It varies from individual to individual. But the ideal that Christ puts before us is that we should set aside anything or anyone or any system, no matter how attractive, that creates a barrier or even an obstacle between us and the friendship of Christ.

The Border

During the war years, I remember visiting some cousins who lived along the Border and was intrigued, though not surprised, to find my aunt religiously blessing with holy water and signing with the cross one of her offspring whom she was dispatching across the fields to smuggle a stone of sugar from the other side. As a truly God-fearing woman, it never occurred to her that she was calling for the blessing of God on what was, according to the law of the land, a crime. To her it was a reasonable and eminently effective solution to a problem created by uncaring politicians in some remote and anonymous city. She wasn't the only one who shared this view. Another cousin pointed out to me years later that it ill behoved us to speak harshly about smuggling, since not a few of us had been reared on the proceeds. Like the war itself, the Border was seen as somebody else's problem.

If they, whoever they were, chose to draw a line between your field and your neighbour's with the intention of separating people who had lived by mutual assistance for generations, and even centuries, it was hardly reasonable to expect you to endorse their craziness. In short, with the patient assurance of country people everywhere who have watched the weeds and the heather eventually reclaim even the most extravagant human follies, they lived as though it were not there and waited patiently for the day when it would no longer be there. And that day has come, in practice if not in theory.

Today we drive nonchalantly past the customs post where you were once subjected to the vigilant scrutiny of customs officers and their chilling enquiry: 'Have you anything to declare?' Sadly, there is the downside to that earthy good sense which carried us through those less than sensible years. The cheerful disregard of distant authority, be it customs officer, government official, police or even clergy, has not always been balanced by a similar sense of individual duty or responsibility.

Even today, we still expect someone in authority to stand over us and take responsibility for decisions that grown-up people might be expected to take for themselves. We have no rule of our own that comes into force when the rules of authority can no longer reach us. We have seen what alcohol can do where there is no inner control, and the failure to police our own lives has left a yawning gap for the inroads of the drugs trade. Economic fraud and business deceit are commonplace in a society that for so long has regarded government as the enemy.

We are still a reasonably Christian people and we like to think that we live our lives according to some basic Christian principles. But there is little point in commemorating the life and death of Christ in Holy Week if we reduce his teaching on personal moral responsibility to the Eleventh Commandment: 'Thou shalt not get caught'.

Like Other Men

'I fast twice a week. I pay tithes of all I get. I give alms to the poor'. That's not bad going for a man whom we profess to despise. He fasts twice a week. I am asked to fast twice a year – Ash Wednesday and Good Friday – but nowadays we regard it as a nuisance, almost an impertinence, to be setting my timetable and making me think about what I can and cannot eat. Of course, I used to fast a lot more when I was younger. Even three days on Lough Derg was no big deal, and in my youth I fasted from midnight every day before receiving Holy Communion. But of late I have grown old and lazy and comfortable. Not this Pharisee. He is no longer young, but he still fasts twice a week and he gives alms to the poor. Well, I give something to Trócaire every year, and I support the St Vincent de Paul Society, and I buy a flag if I am stopped in the street. I don't know that I have much to do with the poor because it is hard to know who is poor nowadays, but I still think I do quite well. So, if this Pharisee can boast about almsgiving, well, so can I. So why, then, did Jesus then find fault with the Pharisee? So far he seems to measure up quite well.

Maybe it's the things he doesn't do or, rather, the people he isn't like. 'I am not like the rest of men, grasping, unjust, adulterers'. Grasping, now there's a wide category of people. He's not far wrong when he includes the rest of men. Have you ever watched a family when there is a dispute about money or land or property? Common sense goes out the window. Parents and children go to war. Brother and sister never speak again. Neighbours start to feud with neighbour and friends become mortal enemies. But I am not like that. I am not grasping. Other people are grasping. I only want my legal rights. But there are grasping people. People who deceive me, tell me lies, play on my sympathy and, dare I say it, on my innocence to get money from me. What about the young man who told me that he was under threat of death from a certain paramilitary organisation because he had given evidence about their activities? He was so convincing. He sat in my reception room and cried his heart out, railed against the injustice of a world which punished the law-abiding and allowed the criminal to go free. He cost me a lot of money, that young man, between fares and accommodation and food, but it seemed the right thing to do at the time. Two weeks later, I saw his photograph in the paper. He was sitting alongside some ardent supporters of the same organisation that had supposedly threatened his life, looking perfectly content.

Oh yes, there are grasping and devious people, and not a bit of wonder the Pharisee didn't want to be like them. The list is endless. 'My mother is in hospital in Dublin and I need the fare to go to visit her'. That usually means 'I've been out drinking with my buddies and we've run out of money'. 'I tripped on a flagstone and I've injured my knee'. That means 'I fell down the stairs when I was intoxicated and I'm looking for a faulty paving stone to blame it on'. 'This coat has a fault in the lining and I want my money back'. This means 'I wore it for a party last night and tore it getting out of the taxi'. Oh yes, there are grasping and devious and ruthless and dishonest people, and not a bit of wonder the Pharisee didn't like them. And what about the unjust? Are they any more likeable? What about the man who skives on the job? He works if you are watching him but not otherwise. And then there is the builder who sees nothing wrong with carrying home your timber or your tools or your cement for his own operation. Or who uses defective materials or shoddy workmanship on your so-called luxury bungalow. Timber so green he has to get the heaviest man in the crew to stand on it before it can be nailed down. Hinges and window catches screwed into place with a hammer.

And what about the adulterers? The grasping, the unjust and the adulterers. There was a time, of course, when the adulterers were very thin on the ground in Ireland. Not that we were any less prone to temptations of the flesh than other nations, but we were very particular about marriage. We believed that a commitment was a commitment. That's not denying that some of them were disasters, vicious and violent relationships that should never have been tolerated. But there was support for the young couples struggling to get their marriage into shape. There was no question of throwing your hat in and walking away because you were bored. But now the young have to cope not only with their own instincts and desires, but also with the bad example of their elders. They see men and women flipping from one relationship to another, regardless of hurt feelings and broken promises. They see husbands and wives cheating on their partners and passing it off as liberated adult behaviour. They see mothers and sometimes fathers left to fend for themselves and their children because they have been abandoned by the other partner. The adulterers are not a very admirable crowd.

The grasping, the unjust and the adulterers. This Pharisee seems to have no liking for the kind of people I wouldn't exactly be dying about myself. So why then did Christ condemn him? He didn't condemn him for what he did but for his attitudes. He thought too much of himself and too little of others. He talked to God like he was God's equal. I have done well here on earth. I kept your laws, so open the gates of Heaven for I'm coming in. And he talked about others as though they were his inferiors. He despised them when in fact he knew nothing about them. This is the heart of the Pharisee's sinfulness. He condemned people without knowing them, just like we do. And we have to resist the temptation to condemn what we do not know and do not understand. We cannot pass judgment on people we do not know. So before we condemn the grasping and the unjust and the adulterers we have to ask ourselves, what do we know about these people? What kind of background and experience made them into the people they are today? Would we have done any better in the same situation? It does not mean that we silently accept and approve their grasping, unjust or adulterous habits. But we see the human being beneath the sinner. And the more we see, the more understanding we become. Their grasping habits may infuriate us, and their unjust ways may anger us, and their adulterous activities may shame us, but we will find excuses for them. Just as we would find excuses for them if they were our own sons and daughters. If we don't get to know them, if we keep our distances, we will either fear or despise them. I remember from my childhood the fear that a classmate of mine had of two little hunchbacked men who used to make a living chopping logs in our town. We often met them pushing their handcart of logs, huge axes over their shoulders, as we made our way home from school. My companion was terrified of them. But I was able to reassure him because they had visited our home and I had talked to them and I knew them. On the other hand, I was terrified of Travellers because my aunt used to tell us when we were young, 'If you don't behave yourself, we will sell you to the gypsies'. And if we met them on the road, it was my companion's turn to reassure me, for he had often met and talked to the Travellers and he had no fear of them. We must not judge or condemn from a distance. That was the Pharisee's sin. We must try to get close so that we may understand better, for God does not see as man sees. Man sees appearances but God looks at the heart. Or, as Abraham Lincoln put it much more forcefully about a man who had sorely tried his patience, 'I cannot stand that man. I really must get to know him better'.

Passion and Death

There is no story as familiar as the story of Christ's Passion and death. In fact, it is hard to believe there ever was a time without that story. But at a certain point in history someone sat down at his desk and said, 'I'd better keep notes of all these stories about Jesus, for a day will come when the people who knew him well will all be dead'. And so he started with the most recent events – the death and resurrection. Who had seen him die? How dependable were they? Was his resurrection a mere propaganda stunt by his followers? Or was there some truth to all the stories? He worked his way back to the public life of Jesus and then to his home life and, finally, to his birth and childhood.

It was an important story, a dramatic story. And the writer wanted people to listen to the story and be moved by it, so he highlighted the various actors in the drama, such as Pilot and Judas and Peter. And he balanced the innocent Jesus with the guilty Barabbas, and the mocking Jewish leaders with the sincere Roman centurion. He even introduced a kind of early shuttle diplomacy, Pilate travelling between the Jewish leaders outside the Praetorium and the solitary Jesus within, trying to find a solution that would be acceptable to the Jews without disturbing his own conscience too much.

Every year we are invited to remember this story and to choose a path that reflects our true feelings about the crucifixion of Christ. Are we part of the crowd that scattered palm leaves before him as he entered Jerusalem in triumph? Or are we more likely to be found among the disciples who abandoned him at the first sign of danger? Does Peter who denied him reflect our true feelings, or maybe we are cast in the image of Judas who betrayed him for money and power? Maybe the fickle Pilate is the truest reflection of our nature, wavering between the demands of truth and the privileges of power, and finally washing his hands to get rid of the blood he has just spilled. Or maybe we would have sided with the religious leaders who wanted Jesus put to death. After all, they were respectable, orthodox, religious people, the kind you will meet in any church today, defending their faith and fighting off the attacks of the godless. We must fit in there somehow. And it would be a sad irony if we found ourselves with the very people who put Christ to death by closing our minds to the possibility of change and the discovery of new life. It is worth remembering that only the dead never change.

'Have it out with him'

Brave words indeed. 'Go and have it out with him alone'. It almost sounds like the old-time invitation to step out into the street and settle this matter once and for all. Except, of course, that Jesus goes on, 'If he listens to you, you have won back your brother'. If a man won't listen to you because you are knocking his block off or he is too busy knocking yours off, then the whole enterprise is a big waste of time. If you are going to correct someone, the whole secret is getting the other man (or woman) to listen.

When I read this lesson from Matthew, I often recall reading in some book or other many years ago, how a respectable, well-to-do businessman is anxious to do more with his life than just make money and to get on. He tries, with the help of a spiritual adviser, to root out the more obvious vices and to leave himself open to the power of God, and he has made fairly good progress. He is working hard. He is giving to the poor. He is praying more frequently and he figures that he is now ready to step a little closer to God, that he is now ready for greater things, and so he tells his spiritual adviser of his ideas. And his spiritual father, being a wise man, says to him, 'I have a little task for you. I want you to go out into the streets of your own town and beg sixpence – that is two and a half pence if you do not belong to the decimal generation'. Naturally, the businessman was horrified. All kinds of embarrassing scenarios swept before his eyes. 'What if one of my children meets me in the street and sees me doing this? What if some of my colleagues at work see me and report me?' As he thought about it, he suddenly realised without anyone telling him that he was far from ready for greater things. Though it must be acknowledged to his credit that he did carry out the assignment. He made it out into the streets in the worst coat he could find and, after having to listen to a couple of lectures from old ladies about the evils of drink and the shiftless modern generation, he made his quota and brought home the sixpence. Now, the question is, why did he obey that spiritual adviser? What persuaded him to risk his respectable, middle-class reputation on such an outrageous venture? I think we must say it was because he trusted him. He was convinced that whatever this man asked him to do would be for his own good. And so he was willing to listen to him.

Now, we are all wonderful advisers and instructors. We will advise you on anything, from your crumbling marriage to the pain in your big toe. We toss out pearls of wisdom like confetti and with about as much effect. We can even get quite violent if you scorn our advice or if you neglect our instructions or disregard our corrections. You will see wives and children and even innocent pedestrians running for cover when we start preaching about how to set the wrongs of the world right. Of course, we would not be the first to try things this way. You remember James and John, the sons of thunder. They were all in favour of lighting a torch under the cities that weren't generous enough with their welcome. 'Shall we call down fire from Heaven?', they asked. And, of course, Peter didn't even ask. When Ananias and Sapphira tried their hand at fiddling the accounts, Peter just struck them down.

Of course, we don't always try the loud and vengeful approach. Sometimes we don't try any approach at all. Or maybe at best we will pluck up our courage and we will follow the example of Eli, the priest. He had two sons who were supposed to help him organise the sacrifices of the Temple. But instead, they used their positions to grab the best of everything. They plunged their three-pronged fork, we are told, into the sacrificial pot and made off with whatever they speared. Eventually, Eli had a quiet word with them but it hadn't the least effect. They were soon back at their badness as if he had never spoken to them. Now, nobody likes to make scenes, especially family scenes, so rather than make a fuss, Eli let things pass. It is the kind of answer we have heard so often before.

'He's my son. I must support him'. But that was where Eli came to grief. For God does not let things pass so easily. Eli and the two boys all died on the one day because he had failed to take a strong hand in correcting them.

So where does the true path of correction lie, if not in roaring anger or in half-hearted complaints? I think the answer is found in the second reading of today's Mass. 'Love', says St Paul, 'is the one thing that cannot hurt our neighbour'. There has to be love in our hearts before we can correct anyone. For without love, we will either shy away from the unpleasant duty, or we will approach it like an avenging fury. Some people offer correction without any thought of the consequences. They toss it out as if they are throwing bones over a fence to a dog. Now, the real Christian knows that he has to climb over the fence with the bone in his hand and risk getting devoured.

When you ask a man to change, you are asking him to perform a painful task. You are asking him to leave behind his familiar and comfortable ways. So, more than likely, he will eat your head off. But that is part of the price you pay for loving someone. He is not rejecting you. He is just expressing his fear of the future. He doesn't want to be left in the lurch like the footballer who was continually being harassed by a supporter. Every time the ball came near him, the supporter called out, 'Go to the left, go to the right, use your head, kick it, swerve', until finally he was caught in a position by the defenders where he could neither go forward, go back, go up or down – he couldn't move at all. He waited to hear what his supporter was going to call this time. And for a long time there was silence. Finally the voice said, 'Use your own judgement'.

If we are asked to change, we want someone to help us to change. Have you ever watched a child that has just been corrected? It might be yelling the house down but it is still holding tightly to the mother who has just smacked it. The bond of love far outweighs the pain of correction. Of course, the opportunities, the real opportunities for correction in our lives will be very few and far between. We really don't get that close to people so often. But if you open your bible at the Book of Proverbs, you will find there that it is scattered with encouragement to take correction, to receive correction, to take correction from wise men. And if you think about it, it does make sense. If a friend is willing to risk that friendship because he has something to say to you, then it would be very foolish of you to let his words pass by without listening to them attentively.

News Review

Newspaper reporters, I am led to believe, will go to extreme lengths to get a headline. But one of them has recently gone a bit far even by their relaxed standards. He has blown the whistle on the whole fraternity, revealing in deathless prose, the schemes, tactics and downright fabrications by which his colleagues make sure that their stories get into print. *Lies, Damn Lies and Some Exclusives* is the name of the book by one Henry Porter. Rather a good name, that, for the job. Hen-ree Porter. And he takes this title from a famous headline in the *Daily Mirror* referring to a 'World Exclusive' which their rivals the *Sun* had splashed across the front pages. It referred to an interview with Mrs Marcia McKay, the widow of Sergeant Ian McKay, who had been awarded a posthumous Victoria Cross for his exploits in the Falklands. There was only one thing wrong with the interview. It had never taken place, because at that moment Mrs McKay was holed up in London with journalists from the *Mirror* giving them an exclusive interview. Naturally enough the *Mirror* was rather miffed about the whole affair and hit back with a fairly trenchant editorial entitled 'Lies, Damn Lies and **Some** Exclusives'.

Of course, it should have come as no surprise to the editors of the *Mirror* to find that the *Sun* was less than spotless in its pursuit of truth. Even that amiable exponent of the frailties of human nature, Norman Stanley Fletcher, has some doubts about its reliability. When he sends his friend Godber to collect the daily papers, he tells him, 'Bring me the *Sun,* and get me something to read while you are at it', or words to that effect. It certainly comes as no

surprise to me to learn that newspapers occasionally invent the
news they print, at least not since that day many years ago when
my father let loose a few unparliamentarily expressions as he read
the local paper, and then proceeded to explain his unusual
behaviour. His friend and colleague, he informed us, was not
merely dead, but buried, and the full account of it, including the
chief mourners and officiating clergyman, was there before him in
the paper. He immediately changed into his best suit and rushed
off to pay his belated respects to the unhappy widow, only to be
met in the doorway by the deceased himself with a lot of cheerful
banter about keeping a careful eye for the rest of his life on friends
who couldn't find time to come to his funeral.

Even the most trustworthy of newspapers can be a victim at
times, whether of inefficiency or fraud, or even a warped sense of
humour, but none of them should invite deception. And they all
do. They are all so anxious for a gripping headline that they are
willing to suspend all their normal cautionary reflexes and accept
some fairy tale as genuine simply because they want it to be
genuine. The most glaring example of this kind of thing was, of
course, the Hitler diaries fraud. The fascinating thing about this
episode was not that the German magazine *Stern* was conned into
believing that the diaries were genuine, nor that the *Sunday Times*
should be persuaded into offering $400,000 for the American and
British rights, but that the *Sunday Times* should be persuaded to do
so before observing any of the normal rules for authentication.
After all, if someone offers you the original stone tablets bearing
the Ten Commandments, you are likely to ask for some proof, even
if you have never touched such a deal before. But the *Sunday Times*
went ahead with the deal even when a leading investigative
reporter, Philip Knightley, pointed out the obvious pitfalls, based
not only on common sense, but also on the paper's own experience
with the so-called Mussolini diaries, which it had foolishly
purchased in the 1960s. Among other things, he mentioned that all
the experts had been wrong in that instance including, and this is
an interesting side-light for students of Irish history, the man who
had authenticated the Casement diaries earlier in the century. Even
Mussolini's son had been wrong about the diaries. And despite

careful negotiations through a leading firm of solicitors, the paper had never recovered a penny of the money it had spent on them. With all this in mind, one would expect the *Sunday Times* to be extremely wary of being caught with the same bait, but caught they were. As Barnum said, 'there's one born every minute'. They didn't actually get into print with the diaries, if my memory serves me, and they didn't lose any money on this occasion, but they dented their credibility considerably and demolished their reputation for reliable journalism for a long time to come.

Of course, it doesn't exactly break my heart to hear of a newspaper being taken to the cleaners. It makes a pleasant change from them taking everyone else to the cleaners. But it makes me wonder, if they can be so easily conned about important things that we would expect them to check out, how much more easily can they be conned about the everyday little titbits of information that fill their pages? Have any of them been checked out? Is there any truth at all in today's papers? Come to that, is there any truth at all in Mr Porter's book and his indictment of newspapers? After all, he is a newspaper reporter himself, and a reporter for the *Sunday Times* at that.

Radio Ulster News Review

The telephone and the doorbell are largely responsible for the fact that I never get peace to read the newspaper at breakfast. Consequently, I have worked out a kind of compromise whereby I read the more serious-minded Sunday papers in instalments, throughout the week. I keep the different sections of these papers at various strategic locations around the house and dip into them when the opportunity arises. The news and political sections still stay in the dining room. The literary section goes to the sitting room, the social section to the bedroom and the business section to the toilet. This last is a hangover from my childhood days when my father, who, as Gerry Anderson would say, was a farmer / cattle dealer, was always on the lookout for someone to drive cattle from one field to another, usually five miles away, and the only way to avoid him was to take a book and hide in the toilet.

I didn't attach any importance to this practice. I mean reading in the toilet. In fact, I gave it a low priority by allocating it the business section. But, as time went by, I found that the business section was a real treasure trove of fascinating, if not particularly significant information. Last week, for instance, I learned that the owner of America's largest house of ill repute, the Mustang Ranch in Nevada, was compelled by the outrageous demands of the taxman to put his business up for sale. The asking price is $18 million, but since the gross daily income is around $25,000, it looks to me, and apparently to a lot of others, because the punters are descending on it thick and fast, like a very sound financial investment. With a twenty per cent profit the business will pay for itself in less than ten years. One thing, however, does worry the potential stockholders. Since it is a crime in most states other than Nevada to live off immoral earnings, they wonder if their earnings might be seen as the fruits of crime, sort of like financing a bank robbery and sharing in the proceeds, and will consequently land them in jail. It would appear, however, that the free enterprise system is held in such high regard, if not awe, in America, that the government cannot bring itself to intervene. This would seem to tally with the contention made in another part of the same business section that it was free enterprise that licked General George Armstrong Custer at the Battle of Little Big Horn. It would appear that some very free and very enterprising trader sold the Indians a load of Winchester sixteen-shot repeater rifles just before the battle and left the unfortunate cavalry to slog it out with single-shot carbines.

Equally fascinating, and also stemming, one feels, from the free enterprise system, is the news that alimony will no longer be the sole privilege of divorced men. In future a divorced wife, if she is in a good financial way of working, will be compelled to pay alimony to her less fortunate husband. To my mind that is a very high price, some would say too high a price, to pay for freedom or equality, or even both.

Now, all these snippets of information comply with my definition of news. They happened but I didn't expect them to happen. I expect wars and famines and earthquakes and plane crashes and all the other calamities that make up the headlines. But they do not really affect me because they are impersonal, far-off events. Anyway, I never get to hear the whole truth about these events. The TV reports are biased by their need for pictures and the newspapers by their need for padding, so I finish up viewing all news with a kind of benevolent cynicism; and then came last week. A friend of mine went missing and I found myself glued to the TV and radio for every news report. They still had all the usual flaws and weaknesses. They got names wrong. They got locations wrong. They even got motives wrong. But they were my only source of information. And when my friend was found – dead as it turned out – it was from a news bulletin that I learned it.

I think in the past week I have come to accept the news as one accepts a friend. I see the faults and the limitations, but I am always conscious of an underlying core of goodness and truth, even if I have to dig deep occasionally to get at it.

Christ the King

The Feast of Christ the Universal King was instituted as recently as 1925. It was, one might say, an imperial title, conferred in the last days of an imperial age; and for that reason, one might safely guess that if the decision were to be taken today, there would be no feast of Christ the King.

The symbolism of kingship is not inappropriate to Christ, but historically monarchy has all but disappeared from the daily experience of most people. Long ago, every land had its king. Even Ireland rejoiced in its monarchy. We not merely had kings, but high kings, a title that we easily transferred to the person of Jesus Christ.

'High King of Heaven, thou Heaven's bright sun' is how Columba addressed him in his famous poem 'Be thou my vision', and down through the ages, the image of Christ as king keeps recurring in Irish religious writings.

'It were my soul's desire, to imitate my King'.

We may, however, be tempted to do away with the feast in our own day because the imperial image of kingly power sits uncomfortably alongside the more topical images of modern democracy and political correctness. If that were to happen, it would be a great loss, because ideas of kingship go way beyond questions of power and influence. The king alone stands above the law, not to abuse it or distort it, but to enhance and fulfil it. When the law has indicted the innocent man, and the law has convicted him, and the law has sentenced him, only the royal pardon of the king can save him from execution.

We need a king to soften the severity of the law. If we are

innocent, we need him to protect us. If we are guilty, we need him to pardon us, for we have no justification to offer for our actions, so we depend entirely on the royal pardon of the king, and that is the kind of pardoner we hope to find in the person of Jesus Christ, King of the Universe; one who pardons not just the innocent victim of the law's ineptness, but the criminal found guilty as charged by the law's impersonal procedure. For we have all sinned and we all need pardon, but we can hope for pardon from Christ because he always put people before the law.

No matter how often his enemies plotted to trip him up with the sin of law-breaking, he always put people first. He healed the sick on the Sabbath in defiance of the law; he defended his disciples who picked ears of corn on the Sabbath in defiance of the law; he sat down at table with tax collectors and sinners in defiance of the law; he forgave the adulterous woman whom the law had found guilty, and he attacked the Pharisees and the lawyers because they loaded the burdens of the law onto people's shoulders without any concern for those who had to bear them. He always laid the emphasis on people rather than procedures, for he knew instinctively that the law is rarely the friend of the truth.

The law concerns itself with legality, not with goodness or beauty or truth, though it hopes to be the servant of all of them. And the complexities of the law can entangle all of us, for good and for bad. Why else would anyone employ the expensive services of lawyers if not to find ways of evading the law and its punishment?

The law is not aimed at making us better people. It is merely concerned with keeping us from becoming worse, or at least from behaving in a worse fashion, and even here it is only occasionally successful; for the intricacies of the law encourage us to become better lawyers rather than better people. When we trip over a faulty paving stone the law does not encourage us to ask, 'How can I rectify this fault so that no one else will trip over it?'; it asks 'How much money can I claim in compensation?'

Christ would have none of this precedence of law over people. He insisted on putting people first, and by doing so he avoided the pit into which the legalist inevitably falls. The ravages of

Nazism and Communism would never have happened, nor would the horrors of more recent years here at home if respect for the individual person had not been suppressed. To Christ, the uniform that people wore did not matter, the slogans they recited did not matter, their racial origins did not matter, their political outlook did not matter, rules and procedures did not matter, even the law of God, handed down through Moses, did not matter if it hurt in any way one of his brothers or sisters. That is the kind of king Christ was; and that is the kind of king I hope to meet on the day of judgment; a king who will look deep into my heart and see there the longing for understanding and love and forgiveness, and who will reach out to me in welcome. What I do not want is a bureaucrat who will confront me with a list of my offences and ask me, 'How do you plead?'

I want to be forgiven for my offences and admitted into a 'grace and favour' home where I can live for eternity. I love that phrase, a 'grace and favour' home. I first heard it on a programme about a man whose family used to live across the lough from here, Field Marshall Montgomery. He asked King George the Sixth for a 'grace and favour' home at the end of the Second World War, but for one reason or another, he was turned down. I hope to be successful. I hope for a king who will not judge me according to the law but who will grant me a royal pardon for all my sins and a 'grace and favour' home where I will live in peace with him forever and ever. Amen.

Dorothy 1–6

PRAYER FOR THE DAY – Dorothy Number 1

Somewhere in the mountainous regions of the old Greek Empire, in the late years of the third century, a young Christian couple looked down with delight and admiration at their newborn daughter, and one of them was eventually moved to say, 'She's a little gift from God'. So that's what they called her 'Dorothy' – 'the gift of God'. She went on to prove herself a true gift of God as she learned more about the faith she was born into, until she found herself giving up her life rather than abandoning it. Legend has it that as she walked to her death, a young man jeeringly suggested that she send him a few flowers from this garden in paradise which, she insisted, she was about to visit. The flowers, of course, duly arrived and the young man eventually found himself following Dorothy's stony path of suffering and death.

Dorothy truly was a gift of God, and as I run my eye down the ages, I am amazed at how many Dorothys truly were the gifts of God, whether feeding the poor or defending the faith or laying bare the secrets of the human condition. This morning's Dorothy proclaims to a hostile world her determination to live out the faith of her childhood, come what may. 'I have fought the good fight. I have finished the course. I have kept the faith'. It is known as integrity. It means living a principled life all the time. It's not easy, but you cannot help admiring it.

'Lord, there are many alluring temptations in my world and many opportunities to pursue them. Put me on my guard against the nice people of this world. They are so much harder to resist than my enemies'.

PRAYER FOR THE DAY – Dorothy Number 2

This morning's gift from God is an American Dorothy, Dorothy Day. Not, please note, Doris Day, but Dorothy Day. I nearly always have to make that correction. Dorothy Day was a journalist, a single mother, a pacifist, a rebel, and a Roman Catholic from the age of thirty. If this were all, she would probably have been forgotten by most people, but she set up what she called Houses of Hospitality, she started a newspaper called *The Catholic Worker*, and she told the president of America and the cardinal archbishop of New York that they were both a disgrace. She was a believer, and in her book true believers spoke out against any injustice. She was jailed for her protest activities but she never sought to defeat anyone, only to convert them. The best, the truest picture of Dorothy Day comes from a journalist who went to interview her, but found her sitting on a doorstep consoling and reasoning with a woman who was very obviously intoxicated. She continued to comfort the woman, patiently listening to a farrago of nonsense, until eventually she turned to the journalist and said, 'Were you waiting to speak to one of us?' That's what I call true Christianity. 'If you do it to one of the least of these brethren of mine, you do it to me'. I would have failed that test.

'Lord, teach us to show respect for one another, especially respect for the so-called losers and the layabouts and the arrogant and the selfish and all those other apparent failures, because if we have no respect for one another, we have no love and if we have no love for one another, we are all lost.'

PRAYER FOR THE DAY – Dorothy Number 3

This morning's gift from God is a silent Dorothy, which makes her the gift of God twice over, for the Book of Ecclesiasticus tells us that 'a silent wife is a gift from the Lord'. This kind of political incorrectness can and frequently does get one into deep trouble, but this morning's Dorothy truly doesn't need to 'contend or cry out or make her voice heard in the streets', for she is Dorothea Lange and she created masterpieces with her camera. Perhaps she had a head start over her competitors because she was stricken with polio as a child and went through her life with a limp. Certainly the experience of suffering can generate compassion, but it won't make you a master craftsman or an artist. Dorothy became an artist when she joined the Farm Security Administration during the Depression and set out to record on film the migrant workers, the sharecroppers and the poor tenant farmers of the American South as they struggled for survival against the wind and the dust. Her photographs did not record the events. They recorded the people and the pain. She had that priceless gift – the photographer's eye – which enabled her to express in an instant what a thousand words would fail to convey.

> 'Lord, help me to understand my enemies. Let me see behind as well as in front of them for I may have missed something important. Help me to look beyond appearances and impressions into the heart of those who are against me, or who think they are against me, because it is my dearest wish that no-one should call me their enemy'.

PRAYER FOR THE DAY – Dorothy Number 4

This morning's Dorothy was a true gift of God for those close to her, but she was a long way from meeting the standards and the expectations of any modern women's liberation movement, and probably failed equally to impress the liberationists of the late eighteenth century, for she was Dorothy Wordsworth, and most of her life was dedicated to protecting and promoting her big brother William, for he, after all, was a poet, and was known far and wide for his poem about the daffodils. So it comes as something of a shock to read in her journal for Thursday 15 April 1802 under the heading 'Inspiration for William' the following words: 'I never saw daffodils so beautiful. They – tossed and reeled and danced and seemed as if they verily laughed with the wind that blew upon them over the water'. Does it sound familiar? Not that old William wasn't grateful. He said nice things about her in some of his poems, but he still went off and married Mary Hutchinson. Even so, Dorothy's life was taken up with William and his poetry. She asked for nothing in return. The joy of being part of an artistic creation was sufficient reward. It might be suggested that submerging one's life in the service of another is the mark of a dullard and a dependant, but no one who has read Dorothy's journals could accuse her of being dull.

'Lord, we sometimes forget that doing good doesn't come naturally; that we have to make conscious decisions whether to love or not to love, whether to serve or not to serve. In whatever decisions we make may we learn to give, and give generously'.

PRAYER FOR TODAY – Dorothy Number 5

Today's gift from God is a Dorothy who might have been happier if God had not been quite so good to her. Dorothy Parker had to carry the burden of genius on fairly narrow shoulders, while projecting an image of hard-bitten unflappability in an age when flappers were the flavour of the day. She sat among the male monuments of the Algonquin Club and matched their stories and their flashes of wit with stories and wit that outshone and outlasted them, but there was always the tension, the dread, of putting pen to paper; not just the writer's natural hatred of the creative process, the willingness to do anything rather than sit down and compose sentences, but the fear that the well will run dry, that the flashes of inspiration will dissipate and decay until you eventually lose your place at the top table, like a poker player who has run out of chips.

Dorothy knew well that behind the glitter of literary success there was simply more glitter – social success, a famous name, financial rewards, and good-time friends, but she stuck with it because she didn't have anything else. Who would love her if she was poor and unknown? So she could only plead guilty to the charge of St Paul that her words had been simply flattery or a cover for trying to get money. She achieved success but she deserved happiness.

> 'Lord, judge the bright people lightly. They brighten our world enormously, but often at a heavy cost to themselves, and help us to make better use of the talents that God has given us. Our present return of thirty per cent is not really good enough'.

PRAYER FOR THE DAY – Dorothy Number 6

This morning's subject is a gift of God whose name is familiar to all readers of detective fiction, Dorothy L. Sayers, the creator of the aristocratic sleuth, Lord Peter Wimsey. She created her ideal man in Lord Peter and tried to fashion a heroine whose initial plainness was offset by a searching mind and a passionate body or, for want of a better description, someone like herself. She had also, not so much a sideline, more a second career as a writer and speaker on religious matters, and she applied the same steely penetration to questions of faith as she did to the intricacies of plot and counter plot. Her starting point was creed, dogma, doctrine or whatever you want to call it. She insisted you must know what you believe. During the war, she gave a talk called 'Creed or Chaos' – imagine filling a hall with that title nowadays – and she pointed out to her audience that if we simply thought that Jesus Christ was just another nice man and nothing more, then the Germans were perfectly entitled to think that Adolf Hitler was a much nicer man and therefore worthy of their support. She cheers me up to no end, for she tackles head on the important question, 'What say ye of Jesus Christ?' For Christians, there is no more important question.

'Lord, do not make us too clever. It gets in the way of belief, for we might start thinking that if we cannot explain the Son of God made man, Jesus Christ, then it cannot be true. Help us to remember that your word is truth'.

Esther 1–6

PRAYER FOR THE DAY – The Plot

It may seem a little bold – if not foolhardy – to suggest that the
Book of Esther sneaked its way into the books of the Bible by the
proverbial skin of its teeth, but it does seem that way, for it was
missing one of the more familiar features of all the other books of
the Bible. It made no mention of God. Instead it talked about fixers
and figureheads, superstars and beauty queens, and dyed-in-the-
wool villains. It was in the days of King Ahasuerus, whose empire
stretched from India to Ethiopia, when he ruled from his royal
throne in the Citadel of Suza. In the third year of his reign, he gave
a banquet at his court for all his administrators and ministers and
chiefs of the army of Persia and Medea. And so it begins. In fact,
the Greek translator felt compelled to give God some mention, so
he added prayers and letters giving all the credit to God, and in
doing so ruined a rather good story. Failing to mention God is not
a fatal omission. Some years ago, a clerical colleague recently
commented on a talk which I had given on local radio. 'He
managed to speak for three minutes without once mentioning
God', he told a friend of mine. I have been sorely tempted to write
to him and say, 'I modelled my style on a man called Jesus of
Nazareth. He frequently spoke for much more than three minutes
without mentioning God'. We will look at these fixers and
figureheads, these beauty queens and superstars and see what they
have to teach us.

'Lord you teach us many important lessons through the works and wisdom of those around us. You created the world and its people and found them all to be good. Help us to see the good in everyone, especially those who do not know you. Amen'.

PRAYER FOR THE DAY – The Figurehead

There is a saying in my part of the country, 'If you have the name of early rising you can lie till dinner time'. Likewise, if you have an air of authority you should never need to use it. But if that is all you have, with nothing to back it up, you will probably live in a state of anxious anticipation, waiting for the first signs of rebellion. In the Book of Esther, King Ahasuerus never quite convinces himself or anyone else that he is in charge. He tries to conceal his anxiety by throwing extravagant parties to impress the regional governors, and by putting on displays of all his precious possessions, even of his wife. 'The king gave a banquet for all the people living in the Citadel of Suza, to high and low alike. On the seventh day, when the king was merry with wine, he commanded the seven eunuchs in attendance on the person of the king to bring Queen Vashti before the king crowned with her royal diadem, in order to display her beauty to the people and the administrators, for she was very beautiful. But Queen Vashti refused to come'. Poor Ahasuerus was humiliated, but even then he wasn't sure what to do. He lay awake at night thinking and wondering. By day he asked this one and that one, 'What do you think I should do about my wife?' He cut a very poor figure indeed as a king.

'Lord you have told us that it is better to confide in God than to have confidence in men, and that it is better to trust in the Lord rather than to trust in princes. Give me the courage to seek your guidance and the confidence to do your will'.

PRAYER FOR THE DAY – The Superstar

We could be forgiven for thinking that superstardom is a modern invention, but in fact it has always been with us. In the ancient world, athletes and gladiators were most likely to get star attention. The winner at the Olympic Games or the champion gladiator in the Colosseum had their groupies and their fan clubs. Even respectable Greek and Roman matrons were reported to be bowled over on occasion by the latest performer. Women, however, had no chance of becoming champions themselves. For them, the path to glory lay in their beauty and their brains. The combination was essential. Beauty alone was not enough to make you a superstar.

The superstar of the Book of Esther is Queen Vashti. She was beautiful and she was smart and she soon got used to unquestioning respect and obedience from all the other women of the kingdom. So was it pride or was it presumption that led her to make the biggest mistake of her career – to defy the king and refuse to appear before him? She forgot that she was living in a man's world and that the man who had lifted her to the heights could now cast her down to the depths, and that is exactly what he did. He had been warned by his advisers that 'the queen's conduct will soon become known to all the women and encourage them in a contemptuous attitude towards their husbands. The wives of the king's administrators will start talking in the same way'. In no time poor Vashti found the credit cards cancelled, the locks changed and her luggage sitting in the street.

'You have made us for yourself, O Lord, and so we are all precious in your sight. Support and encourage all those who find themselves neglected, unloved or forgotten. Help them to find their true selves and in their true selves to find peace'.

PRAYER FOR THE DAY – The Beauty Queen

As you might reasonably expect, Esther is the heroine of the Book of Esther, and as befits a heroine, she is now married into a royal family, the family of the Medes and the Persian; but less typically she has launched her career by winning a beauty contest. The former Queen Vashti had been sacked for disobedience and the king invited all the beautiful girls in the kingdom to apply for the job. 'Each girl had to appear in turn before King Ahasuerus. And the king liked Esther better than any of the other women: none of the other girls found so much favour and approval with him. So he set the royal diadem on her head and proclaimed her queen'.

Esther was never comfortable with her looks or her position. Like many beautiful women, she found her beauty a burden as well as a benefit, for it both attracted and repelled people. For some she was an exotic goddess, inaccessible to all but the richest and most powerful. For others she was a warm light drawing all kinds of creatures into her ambit. She could never be sure if they were drawn to her beauty, or if they were drawn to her power or if they were just good friends who wanted nothing but the best for her. So she opted for duty. She would follow the guidance of her cousin Mordecai for he was her guardian in God's eyes, and she would do what best served her people, no matter how distasteful.

'Lord, we pray to you each day, 'Thy will be done on earth as it is in Heaven'. Yet we often forget that we alone have the power to make your will happen in this world, to see that the good and generous thing is done rather than the evil thing. Help us to be faithful Christians in word and in deed'.

PRAYER FOR THE DAY – The Villain

Every good story has a villain and the Book of Esther leaves us in no doubt about who he is. If the story had been a Western, Haman would have been dressed in black clothes and a black hat. Haman was a foreigner, a man who had worked his way up the promotion ladder to become head of the civil service, but the author leaves us in no doubt that he was a very dangerous man. And if someone didn't stop him, he would wipe out the entire Jewish nation. Haman said to King Ahasuerus, 'There is a certain nation scattered throughout your realm; their laws are different from those of all the other nations and ignore the royal edicts; hence it is not in the king's interest to tolerate them. If it pleased the king to decree their destruction, I am prepared to pay two thousand talents of silver to the royal treasurer'. That was a lot of money, but it was a small price to pay for the property and possessions of the entire Jewish nation – which was Haman's ultimate objective. And the really sad aspect of Haman's behaviour was that it was motivated by personal rancour. Everyone showed due deference to Haman except Mordecai, the leader of the Jews, and this seemed to eat into Haman's soul. If even one man could despise him, then he was still a nobody, and a foreign nobody at that. If it was going to take the destruction of the entire people to make him feel important, then so be it. The story has a frighteningly familiar ring to it.

> 'Lord, you know how deluded we can be by the pursuit of power and possessions and how ludicrous our pretensions to grandeur can be. Help us to expand and develop the talents you have given us and find greatness in our hearts and not in our possessions'.

PRAYER FOR THE DAY – The Fixer

The fixer in the Book of Esther is the leader of the Jewish people, Mordecai. This might seem a rather harsh title to bestow on a man who carried responsibility for a whole nation on his shoulders. Perhaps 'manager' or 'organiser' would be a better word, but there was a touch of deviousness and occasionally a touch of ruthlessness about Mordecai that persuaded people to step carefully around him. When his enemy Haman persuaded the king to permit the destruction of the Jews, Mordecai did not hesitate to put pressure on his cousin Esther to risk her life by approaching the king uninvited and pleading for her people. 'Do not suppose that, because you are in the king's palace, you are going to be the one Jew to escape. No; if you persist in remaining silent at such a time, relief and deliverance will come to the Jews from another place, but you and the house of your father will perish'. In fact, Mordecai rose to prominence on the shoulders of his cousin Esther. He was just another Jewish captive until Esther was chosen by the king for his harem. And we are told that Mordecai walked up and down in front of the courtyard of the harem every day to learn how Esther was being treated, and also, I imagine, to hear the latest gossip. Shortly afterwards, we find him attached to the chancellery, and from there he was able to keep an eye on his colleagues and report anyone who stepped out of line. Yes, I think fixer is the correct word.

> 'Lord, we live in a sinful and often violent world and have frequent need of your help. Guide us by your spirit to use the talents you have given us to become models of probity and peace to all those we encounter'.

The Most Endangered Species

Another endangered species is hardly headline news. But I think it's fair to say that this one's different and does concern you and me directly. The problem with the whales and the buffaloes and the giant pandas is that they are all a long way from home – our home, that is. And we don't usually get hot under the collar about what is happening in the Arctic Ocean or the bamboo forest of China. In fact, we have lived in blissful ignorance of these places for a lot of years. But of late we have been bombarded with so much information about ecology that now there is a danger that we will stop listening through sheer boredom. That danger also exists for anyone talking about the preservation of the human animal. But I will take a chance that there is still something new to be said about the ultimate endangered species, man himself, the human race.

On the face of it, I know that sounds like a ludicrous idea, that the human race is in danger of extinction, especially since everyone else is worrying about the population explosion. But I am not joking. I do sincerely believe that man could wipe himself off the face of the earth if he keeps going the way he is going today. And it won't be with nuclear bombs or chemical weapons or the latest laser technology, for the simple reason that these weapons were never intended to kill people, and I will explain that crazy idea a little later.

One thing we learned from the whales and the buffaloes and the pandas was that no kind of natural disaster was ever likely to wipe them out. Earthquakes, forest fires, drought, disease, famine and flood could all come and go and at least a few would survive. It is only when man got to work with sophisticated killing techniques that any species was in danger.

Nobody stopped them at the time because everyone thought there was a limitless supply of these animals. In North America, the buffalo herds stretched as far as the eye could see, and the whaling fleets of South Georgia were towing huge catches into the island's six processing plants, so recently that one can see movie film of it in colour, and never a voice raised in protest. However, when the repeating rifle and the exploding harpoon got to work among them, their days were numbered. So, on the basis of experience, I maintain that the present population of the world is no guarantee whatever that we cannot all be wiped off the face of the earth given the right conditions.

War, in the traditional sense, has been quite successful, especially in the past eighty years, in wiping out vast numbers of the human race. It has probably accounted for about one hundred million in this century alone. But, as I have said, these deaths were mostly accidental or incidental. The real purpose of war is not to kill. It is to conquer. If one side in a war were to lay down its arms and surrender, there would hopefully be no killing at all. So, strictly speaking, we cannot rely on wars to wipe out the human race. There was, however, one event in the Second World War, not necessarily connected with it, which did not fit into this theory, and that was the killing of the Jews. Here the intention was to kill, not to conquer, or scatter or enslave, but to kill, so it didn't matter what a Jew did in the last war. He might hand over all his property. He might get down on his knees and kiss the feet of his conquerors. He might even betray his comrades and work for the Nazis, but eventually he was going to die because that was Hitler's intention, to kill all the Jews. Now, we have seen the gruesome excesses that this intention led to. So, it is reasonable to assume that where men deliberately set out to kill their fellow men with the approval and blessing of the state, there will be no holds barred. Everyone will finish up in the melting pot, if you will excuse the expression. Old and young, guilty and innocent, men, women and even the babies in arms will all die.

Now, as the Nazis discovered, the technology for killing and disposing of large numbers was very clumsy, involving as it did so many bulky physical bodies. And right to the end they were searching for efficient ways of disposing of their victims. The obvious answer was to get them before they grew into bulky adult human beings. Or better still, to get them even before they were born, when they were tiny, unable to hide, and unable to fight back. Fortunately, the war ended before they were able to implement the final solution. But their methods and their ideas did not die with them. And we now live in a world where your chances of survival are little better than a Jew in wartime Germany. I don't know the figures for Ireland, but your chances of survival in America are about fifty/fifty. In other words, you are just as liable to be killed in the womb before you are born as you are to survive.

Now this, of course, is where the arguments and the objections begin. Abortion isn't the same as killing children. It is not a child until it is born and so on. Well, as Cardinal Spellman answered when someone asked him why he branded a certain group as Communists, he said, 'If it looks like a duck and waddles like a duck and quacks like a duck, I call it a duck'. And a foetus from its very early days looks and moves and behaves like a child, so I call it a child. I don't care what the US Supreme Court has said about it. In fact, some of the things they have said about it have convinced me that the welfare of the human race should not be entrusted to lawyers. They deal in the letter of the law and forget about the spirit. And that's what we are, body and spirit, not body and law. Even at a legal level, I am not impressed with their judgments. The least one expects in a legal document is the clear-cut and precise expression of ideas. Instead we get sloppy verbiage such as 'potential life'. One might as well talk about potential death. And the word 'viable', which they define as 'capable of meaningful life'; one has no right to live unless one is capable of meaningful life. It would seem, then, that the next time someone gets stuck in a pothole or trapped in a coal pit, the only thing to do is to leave them there because they certainly cannot lead a very meaningful life in a hole thousands of feet underground. Of course, one could always give some meaning to their lives by hauling them up again. But this does not seem to have occurred to the Supreme Court. However, there is no point in pursuing all the arguments for and against, because most people have already made up their minds about abortion. And whether the foetus is or is not a child does not seem to affect their behaviour when the chips are down. As one lady said, explaining her abortion, 'I believe it is a human being all right, but if I let it live I will get stretch marks and I won't be able to wear my bikini'. So a baby dies because mammy wants to be what we are told every modern women hates to be – a sex symbol. Anyway, we are not going to save babies by proving to their mothers that they are human beings, even before they are born. We can, however, learn a lesson from the endangered animals and apply it to this situation with better hope of success.

Every year thousands of seal pups were slaughtered for their fur and the justification for it was that there were too many of them and they would devour all the fish. The conservationists argued against this and said they weren't too many of them but nobody paid any attention. It was only when they highlighted the fact that the seal hunters were beating the pups to death with baseball bats that they caught the public attention and forced through at least a partial restriction on the killing. Well, I cannot hope to convince you by argument of the wrongness of abortion, but I have faith in the opposition of any fair-minded person to cruelty to animals, and that, I think, will be enough to swing public opinion around once your know the facts.

All animals are protected from cruelty by law and there is a full-time body to ensure that the law is enforced. Even animals which have to be killed for food, and stray or abandoned animals which have no-one to care for them, must be killed in as painless a way as possible. The unborn infant, however, has no such protection. It can be put to death with any degree of cruelty and the law of the land will not say a word.

Briefly there are four methods of abortion. Sharp curettage, suction curettage, saline solution and prostaglandins or, to express it more simply, the foetus can be cut up, sucked up, pickled or suffocated. The first method simply dices the child into small pieces with a sharp knife and removes it piece by piece. The whole process takes about ten minutes. The second sucks the child into a kind of vacuum cleaner, but again the child is too big to emerge in one go so it must be pulled apart and sucked through in pieces. Again, it takes about ten minutes for the whole operation. Incidentally, if you have any doubts about the painfulness of this method I can refer you to a friend of mine who was sucked into the engine of a jet fighter on an aircraft carrier. He escaped with his life through the prompt action of his companions but only just. The third method involves injecting a salt solution into the fluids surrounding the foetus. I am not quite sure how it kills the child but it takes about two hours and I am told that the aborted foetus looks like it had been soaked in acid. If some of the solution gets into the body of the woman accidentally during the operation it can be extremely painful. I will leave it to your imagination to figure out what it must be like to be soaked in it for two hours. The fourth method uses natural body chemicals to produce an unnatural effect, labour and birth at sixteen weeks. The circulation and the functioning of the heart are both impaired by the process, and if you have asthma or a bad heart you will know how painful that can be.

So there you have it. You and I were lucky. We survived the killing round, but for millions the killing has only begun. If a little animal were being cut to pieces you and I would recoil in horror from its screams. Isn't it strange that we can tolerate the infliction of similar cruelty on little children simply because we cannot hear the screams?

Genetic Engineering

There are few subjects I know less about than genetic engineering, so maybe that is why the little I have read about it over the years has scared me so much. If you have never heard of it, then do not be at all surprised, because the people who work at this kind of thing tend to hide their light under a bushel – at least until the flame is well and truly blazing. Like all kinds of engineering, it is concerned with creating some new object from the bits and pieces of daily life. A good engineer starts out with familiar materials and ideas and assembles them in a new order, and the result is a new kind of car, or skyscraper or whatever. Of course he can also finish up with a new kind of gun or bomb or nuclear missile, and that is why we need to look over their shoulders now and then and see what is happening.

Until recently, genetic engineers were a perfectly harmless breed of men – at least by comparison with other professions – for whatever they made was harmless in itself. It had to wait for some other man to come along and use it before it could produce any result – whether good or bad. But not so any longer. The genetic engineer doesn't work with steel or bricks. He works with living organisms, reassembling the bits and pieces of living things in a new order, so that he ends up with a different item – a new form of life. Now I have nothing against exploring the mysteries of human life, but having driven some of the cars that engineers have put together, I am not so sure I want to share my bed with some of the new life forms they may come up with.

When genetic engineering started out, it was relatively harmless. It concerned itself mostly with plant life, and it came up with a few ideas that were beneficial to the human race. For instance, it developed new varieties of plants that were more productive and more resistant to disease, and that in itself improved the food output of the world enormously.

However, it was not long before the transition was made from plant to animal life, and things grew a little more complicated, though it was still fairly harmless. The same principles were applied, and soon we had horses that ran faster, and hens that laid more eggs, and cows that gave more milk, and everybody was very pleased. Of course, there were some unforeseen problems, such as the turkeys that were so heavy that they could not engage in any kind of sexual activity and had to be artificially fertilised, and there were complaints about some methods, such as battery feeding and manipulating the lights so that the poor hens were conned into laying more eggs, but nothing too serious.

The last decade, however, has seen the pace of research speeding up like never before, and just a few years ago there was a very significant breakthrough. Like so many other things today, it all started with oil. The oil business is so vital to modern life that anything that affects it is given very careful examination. You may recall that there were several unhappy incidents involving oil in recent years, such as large tankers running up on the rocks or banging into one another on the open sea, and the resultant oil spillage made some people very angry indeed. Now the last thing the oil companies want is to have people angry with them, so they immediately hustled to find a way of clearing up the mess, and getting people to love them again.

Their first efforts were not too successful. They treated the ocean like a huge sink full of dirty dishes and poured tons of detergent into it, but who wants to go swimming in soapy water? As any child will tell you it is bad enough having to wash in it. The second solution was a little better, but it was clumsy and a bit messy. The oil slick was lassoed with a huge boom like a floating sausage and the noose tightened so that the oil could be scooped up into the ship again.

And then came Mr Ananda Chakrobarty with his solution – and it was as brilliant as it was unlikely. Mr Chakrobarty is a scientist and he worked out a process whereby 'four different plasmids, capable of disintegrating four different components of oil, could be transferred and maintained in a bacterium which itself had no capacity to disintegrate oil'. Now, if you are like me and you do not know a plasmid from a hole in the ground, you may wonder what the last sentence meant. Well, translated into English it means that Mr Chakrobarty adjusted a whole lot of little microbes, millions and millions of them, so that they would eat oil for their dessert instead of rice pudding or whatever they had been having up till then. As soon as there was an oil spill he took all his pet bacteria out to the spot and unleashed them and they gobbled up the spill and left the seas clear and shining again. Where they went and what they did after they had dessert is another question, but everyone was very pleased with Mr Chakrobarty, and the US Supreme Court thought so highly of him that they allowed him to patent his invention. This might seem a very reasonable thing to do, but in fact it was an even bigger breakthrough than the invention itself, for up till then a lot of scientists had been opposed to the idea of patenting any formula for creating new genetically engineered life forms. Many of them saw it as a threat to the human race, or at least, tending to depreciate the value of human life. The Supreme Court evidently thought otherwise, and Mr Charkrobarty is now in the happy position of being able to charge a licence fee for any use of his formula to create these little creatures, and with oil tankers still dotting the oceans like seagulls, it seems that there will be plenty of demand for them, at least in the foreseeable future.

That was the first real example of genetic engineering – up to then it had been more like selective breeding – so it came as no surprise to discover that the scientists were now beginning to experiment with human life. It was not exactly new ground, for even Hitler had tried his hand at it in the concentration camps; but today's scientists were not anxious to have their names linked with such unsavoury company so, for one reason or another, their early experiments were concerned with helping to create life when the human mechanism had broken down in some way. Their work was all lumped together under the misleading heading of test-tube babies, and involved finding a way of fertilising the human ovum or egg outside the body and then transferring it back to the womb where it could grow to full maturity. Naturally enough there was great triumph and rejoicing when Louise Brown – the first test-tube baby – was born, but then somebody started asking questions about the procedures involved. They wanted to know, for instance, how many eggs had been fertilised, and what the doctors had done with the extras, and whether there were other people doing this same kind of experiment, and so on, and eventually it came to light that a whole lot of doctors were doing this kind of work and a whole lot of eggs were being fertilised without any record of where they came from. Some of them were being frozen for later use, but others were being flushed down the toilet. This began to worry a lot of people, because if one child had begun life in a test-tube, then it seemed reasonable to assume that all these other fertilised eggs were children in miniature too, and it did not seem proper to go flushing little children down the toilet – no matter how undeveloped they were. In fact, one American lady successfully sued her doctor for $50,000 for doing just that.

That was just one cause for concern, but already there was a new and far more alarming possibility looming on the horizon. If it was possible to fertilise human eggs in a glass dish with human sperm, maybe somebody would try to fertilise a human egg with animal sperm, and then what would happen? If it succeeded, it might be possible to bring to full term this new being, half man and half monkey, or whatever.

Now, of course, there are no laws to govern such experiments. It is part of the human condition that laws only come into operation when things are beginning to get out of hand. For example, it was only when roads got choked up with traffic that governments imposed speed limits and driving tests and so on.

However, there is a big difference between cars and human beings, and if human lives are at stake then obviously the law must provide some protection for them right away; but nobody really knows enough about these things to make effective laws – at least not yet – so the individual doctor or scientist is free to make his own decision. The Medical Research Council drew up some guidelines, which in effect approved the experiments and merely suggested that the fertilised eggs should not be allowed to develop beyond the early cleavage stage – that is when the cell splits up and begins to multiply. Now, without casting any slur on the medical profession, I think it a bit optimistic to assume that they will all resist temptation when the occasion of sin arises. Indeed, one of their own members admitted that only the fear of public reaction had so far kept them from pursuing their experiments further. If that is so, then we can shortly expect to find that someone who is not so sensitive to public opinion will carry the operation through to the bitter end, and produce a creature that is part-man part-animal; and, believe it or not, some scientists are already making soothing noises about the possible advantages of having, say, an intelligent chimpanzee about the house to do the boring work, like washing the dishes or mowing the lawn, though so far nobody has mentioned the money that can be made by the man who patents the formula for producing these cheerful little nightmares.

Perhaps you think I am reaching too far, and wandering off into the realms of science-fiction. Well, try this one for size, as the Americans say. Scientists have already succeeded in fertilising the ovum of a hamster with a human sperm, and if it did not grow beyond the early cleavage stage, it was because they did not know how to keep it alive and not because of any moral principles. But given time, they will learn how to keep it alive; so in years to come if your pet hamster steps off his little wheel, looks you in the eye, and says, 'What's up, Doc?', do not say I did not warn you.

The brave new world is well and truly on its way.

Non-verbal Communication

Three hundred years ago, at the end of the twenty-third century, in the year AD 2280 to be exact, verbal communication was finally discarded from the universal education system. The immediate cause was the mass production and widespread use of the total awareness transceiver, a miracle of microtechnology in its day, but the writing was already on the wall for many years beforehand. The use of words, either in printed or spoken language, was so obviously inefficient and inaccurate that today we can only wonder that an alternative was not sought much earlier. The suggestion has been made that men were in love with words. That they had honed and fashioned them into such beautiful shapes and combinations down the centuries that they lost interest in their efficiency and accuracy. In the same way as some men maintained and treasured old steam engines long after they had gone out of use, others maintained and treasured words, even when alternative techniques of communication were available. At any rate, words continued to be the everyday means of communication, even in the midst of the scientific advances of the twentieth and twenty-first centuries, and it is only by recreating, in a way that I will explain later, the conditions and the limitations of that bygone age, that we can have any idea of the difficulties men faced and understand the mistakes they made before the communication problem was finally solved.

The heart of the problem lay in words and their meaning. Everyone used the same words. But everyone gave them a different meaning. Frequently, an individual gave a word a different meaning each time he used it. Everyone spoke of 'peace', for example. But everyone had his own definition of peace. What was 'cheap' to one was 'dear' to another, even though both were talking about the same thing. And to describe something as 'dear' could mean that it was either lovable or expensive, two completely different concepts.

This was merely the tip of the iceberg, for the confusion really multiplied when men were confronted by others who spoke a different language. Inevitably, this confusion gave rise to misunderstanding, and misunderstanding in turn gave rise to all kinds of problems. Vast sums of money and vast amounts of time and energy were spent in dealing with these problems. Such things as war, famine, poverty, crime, corruption, hatred, jealousy and fear, indeed every evil known to man, was traceable to this inability of the human race to express itself clearly. We might, of course ask, 'What about greed and ambition? Surely they were responsible for some of the problems that man was facing?' Not really, because the greedy or ambitious man could only succeed if he concealed his intentions by using deceptive words. The starting point was always the relationship between two people. A. said something to B. Because he was unsure of himself, or because he had a deprived childhood, or a funny nose, or because he was dishonest; for one reason or another, he conveyed something in his words that was not intended and aroused the suspicion or anger or fear of B., who immediately got very defensive in his response. This situation was aggravated when their friends joined the conversation. And it was merely a matter of time before confusion expressed in words gave way to confusion expressed in action, which is another of describing international war. So wars were fought and both sides had exhausted themselves and their resources before they realised the madness of it all and laid down their arms. Behind them, in the meantime, another generation also failed to understand one another and prepared to repeat the performance all over again.

Meanwhile, the behavioural sciences were still in their infancy. But once the problem was tackled, and the initial premise accepted that verbal communication was inaccurate because communication was an activity of the whole person, it was merely a matter of time before a new method of communication was invented. Scientists had already coined the term 'body language', which at least showed their awareness of the complexity of communication. They studied reflex actions of the body, such as blushing, sweating, fidgeting of arms and legs, facial activity – especially eye movement – and using this knowledge, they were able to exercise a certain amount of control over their subjects by applying suitable stimuli. They found, for example, that by playing soft music in supermarkets, they could reduce the shopper to a semi-comatose state, indicated by an abnormally slow blink rate of the eye, so that he or she wandered around the store, dreamily picking item after item from the shelves without showing any of their usual concern about quality and price. This kind of expertise was very convenient for those who could read body language, but it meant that those who could not were wide open to exploitation. It was important that some method or machine be developed, whereby everyone would be able to read not just the external signs but also the internal thoughts and sensations of others, without fear of error.

It was the early part of the twenty-second century before such a machine was invented, the Total Awareness Transceiver, or TAT, as it was then called. It consisted of a kind of skullcap containing twelve electronic sensors which fitted exactly over the twelve nerve centres of the brain, surmounted by a small directional aerial, and linked to a powerpack and transceiver which could be clipped to the belt or fitted into a pocket. The wearer had only to face someone wearing a similar device and the entire thought and sensation process of each could be transmitted to the other without any intervening words. Naturally enough, there was considerable resistance to its use. Few men were ready or willing to reveal their entire thought processes to anyone else. But the unanswerable argument was that only those with something to hide would be unwilling to use it. Over the years, it was refined and perfected, and by the year 2280, it had finally been accepted as the basis of the universal education system. It did not make learning any easier, but it made it more accurate and efficient.

A mere forty years later, scientists working in the International

Research Centre in Northern Kenya succeeded in miniaturising all the functions of the TAT, siting them in a small disc, a mere centimetre in diameter and a millimetre in thickness. It was powered by body heat, and by making a small incision in the skin of the skull it could be inserted and left there for a lifetime. Its performance was so impressive that by the year 2400, universal law decreed that everyone should have it inserted within one week of birth. It was the ultimate victory of the machine over man. Or so it seemed.

It overlooked 'Murphy's Law', a tarnished little pearl of wisdom from the twentieth century which stated that if it can go wrong, it will go wrong. Theoretically the TAT was perfect, but the inevitable carelessness of man slipped into its manufacture, and defective equipment gradually began to appear. The novelty of unsupervised thought was rediscovered, and small groups sprang up who were openly opposed to the TAT, claiming the right of every man to live his own life, what they called the right to privacy. A flourishing black market in TATs soon followed. And with no effective means of monitoring the mental processes of large sections of the population, it soon became clear that, barring some revolutionary breakthrough in communication, there would be universal anarchy.

The final solution, one that we accept as part and parcel of modern life, was neither startling nor revolutionary. It had been sitting under our noses, so to speak, all the time. It had been known for centuries that some individuals had the power to send and receive messages over vast distances without any mechanical aids. It was variously called 'telepathy' or 'extrasensory perception' And one day, someone asked a rather obvious question. 'Why can everyone not do this?'

The answer was simple. Because only a select few carried in their bloodstream a minute amount of a hitherto unknown chemical, Biotel 4. The rest is history. By adding a tiny amount of Biotel to the water supply, everyone acquired this rare gift. And with a little practice, everyone was soon able to direct their thoughts at will in any direction and over any distance. It is such a commonplace of our way of life, that in order to recreate the limitations of verbal communication, I activated a sonic filter, a kind of jamming device, before speaking to you today, so that you would be compelled to rely on verbal communication alone. Historians tell us that although our ancestors acknowledged the beneficial effects of the first thought-transfer systems, the end of corruption and crime and eventually of wars and violence, they resented the abolition of many intimately human pleasures, such as literature and live theatre, not to mention the indefinable pleasure of bluffing an opponent in a simple game of cards. Whether we have advanced or restricted the happiness of man, I must leave you to be the judge.

Contemplation

I am haunted by the face of a man I have never seen. He is a Jew called Abraham – not the one in the Bible; this one is very much alive, and his home is on the side of a mountain on the outskirts of Athens. The story of his life is so fantastic as to be unbelievable, and the story of how a man living on the side of a mountain in Greece came to share his story with a young girl living on the side of a mountain in County Derry is another and equally fantastic tale. However, that is for another day. For the moment I just want to focus on one aspect of Abraham's life.

Like all European Jews of his day, he was caught between the glorious promises of his God and the irrational viciousness of his neighbours. He is a patriarchal figure now, with his flowing white beard and long robe. He spends his days tending his goats and his garden and it is comparatively easy to accept the long hours that he spends each day in prayer. We expect old men to be holy. But for Abraham, it was always so. Even in his youth he went twice to the synagogue every Sabbath. He prayed and did penance every Friday evening. He gave the best portions of his crops and his herds to the rabbi. He sprinkled himself before eating. He set a place at table for the unknown guest and, to the best of his ability, he carried out the rites and observances of his faith handed down by his ancestors. He rejoiced in his privileged position as one of God's chosen people and never doubted that God kept a special eye at all times on himself and all the other members of his race.

Then came the war and with it the German invasion of Greece, but he was not afraid. God would provide. When the Germans told them, through their own leaders, that the Jews would be resettled in a new land until the war was over, he had no difficulty believing them. It was the hand of God again, reaching out to save his own people from the destruction around them. When they told him he would have to pay for his ticket, he sold everything he owned except a few pieces of jewellery that had been handed down from generation to generation and, with his new wife, he boarded the train – for Auschwitz.

During his years in the concentration camp, Abraham underwent every kind of privation and degradation. There was no logic or reason to his existence. Neither hard work nor good behaviour could guarantee him an extra moment of life; he prayed that God would spare him, so that one day he could set foot outside the gate of the camp. Even if he died a second later, it would not matter; he would have beaten his enemies; he would be free again. There was, however, one huge problem – his freedom to pray had been taken from him too. The Jews have a very distinct and vocal style of prayer. They stand before God with their heads covered, reciting the ancient psalms and prayers in a curiously dirge-like melody. It is a public act of worship, almost a community act, with little or no room for innovation or privacy. For Abraham, all that was gone. He had to leave behind the tradition of his forefathers and speak to God in the silence of his heart.

Abraham's face haunts me because he lost everything. His was the story of Job all over again, right down to the repulsive sores on his body, and yet he never lost faith. When his customary path to God was blocked, he did not give up, but he searched until he found a new and better way. One could say that God drove him by a hard road, and it makes me feel bad to know that I could make the same discovery so much more easily but I have not done so.

And I feel worse when I see the vast numbers of people in this bustling business-like world of ours who are trying to make this same discovery and have no one to lead them. Whether they call it finding God, or finding happiness or finding peace is of no importance. They are all searching for meaning and stability in their lives, and whether they know it or not, they are searching for God.

A generation ago if you talked about meditation or mysticism, you were presumed to be an enclosed monk or a crackpot. Contemplation was rated alongside listening to classical music. There might be a few genuine devotees who enjoyed it but the others were merely doing it to impress you, a kind of cultural or spiritual one-upmanship. Now everything has changed. A world that has all the technology and gadgetry of the nuclear age at its fingertips is crying out for some meaning to this crazy life, and it is not only the dropouts and the poets who are looking into their souls. Right out in the vanguard are the scientists who have tired of their machinery and are turning back to man himself as the only mystery still worthy of their attention.

From all this has come a resurgence of interest in methods of contemplation. The popularity of yoga, zen, transcendental meditation, even of sports such as karate and judo, can all be traced back to the need in man for some permanence, some discipline in his life, instead of being battered and shaken by every wind of change that blows his way. Those who put their hopes in power or money, material goods or the infinite potential of medicine, have all been disappointed. They walled themselves in with their worldly possessions, but unhappiness seemed to climb over the wall without the least difficulty.

The alternative was to develop an immunity to misery, an interior defence that would repel the very worst the world could throw at them. It was hoped to find it in the very old yet very new science of meditation, so they turned to the East, especially to India and Japan, and one of the leaders of this search was, surprisingly enough, a Belfast man called William Johnston. He studied mystical theology in Tokyo and later joined the staff there, a case of teaching your granny to suck eggs if ever there was one. He learned the hard way, doing such things as ten-day retreats where you sat cross-legged for forty minutes out of every hour, ten hours a day. But he was able to encourage the growing dialogue between the monks of the Buddhist faith and the scientists.

It was not that they expected the scientists to tell them anything new or startling about the different states of mind that came with meditation, but they could use their skills to study the effect of these states on the brain, which they did, and came up with some very useful information. As early as the 1920s, a German scientist, Hans Berger, had discovered brainwaves and their relation to varying states of consciousness. So, by hooking up a new machine to the brain, the new scientists were able to determine what state of awareness the subject had reached by observing the pattern of his brainwaves.

For convenience, brainwaves are usually divided into four groups according to their frequency. First there are beta waves, measuring thirteen or more cycles per second, which occur when we are thinking or concentrating our attention on anything. Traced onto paper the waves reflect the state of mind of the subject. They are tight, fussy little waves full of tension and hurry. Alpha waves are more restful, occurring at about eight to twelve cycles per second and they reflect a state of relaxed awareness. We know what is going on but we're not too concerned about it. On paper they show up as a much smoother line with wider spaces between each wave and fewer jagged edges. Below that we have theta waves, which occur at four to seven cycles per second and indicate drowsiness, and then delta waves at the bottom of the scale, which indicate that you are asleep.

To pursue their experiments the scientists simply invited some Buddhist monks into their laboratory, hooked up a few electrodes to their brains and asked them to pray. Almost immediately, the brainwaves slowed down to a nice gentle alpha as the monks entered a state of distractionless meditation. Then, for the sake of comparison, they invited some Catholic clergymen to pray. It was a catastrophe. They read the Bible, sang hymns, walked around the room, sent jagged beta waves bouncing off the scale and generally fouled up the machinery. It was only when they extended the scope of their experiments to include some Carthusian monks that the reputation of the Christian tradition was salvaged.

It was a confirmation of what the eastern nations had always observed about western missionaries. They couldn't help but admire their social consciousness and their charitable works, but they could never figure out when these 'holy men' prayed. That there are more distractions from prayer in the world today is obvious to everyone, and that there is a need for this kind of prayer is proved by the fact that at a recent talk in Termonbacca Retreat Centre, entitled 'Basic Techniques of Meditation', over a hundred people turned up. Maybe God will have to drive us down Abraham's long hard road before we discover it, which would be a pity, because it is there waiting for anyone who wants to make use of it.

Resurrection

On this Easter Day, I am tempted to begin by saying that we celebrate today the greatest feast of the Christian Church, on the unwarranted assumption that you know all about Christ and his Church; and that may be a gross liberty on my part. If the student intake of an Oxford College for one year can, despite all its intellectual brilliance, have no idea of the historical or spiritual significance of Good Friday, it may be a bit rash of me to assume that you already know all about Easter Sunday.

And yet, I think I would be disappointed if I could find a single primary three schoolchild in Northern Ireland who could not link Easter Sunday and the resurrection of Jesus Christ from the dead. While we have gained an unenviable reputation abroad for our religious intolerance, we do generally tend to take more care than most that our children will know at least the facts of the Christian faith, but that little bit of learning in religion can often turn out to be a dangerous weapon in the hands of the fanatic. Knowledge is not faith, and even the devil can quote scripture for his own purposes. We have to acquire the humility that leads to faith, if we are to grow from knowledgeable pupils into faithful Christians.

The resurrection of Jesus Christ is indeed the central and crucial event of the Christian faith, but it is an unbelievable story to begin with, and that makes it particularly difficult to establish as a believable fact. If it were a less outlandish claim it might be easier to believe; but perhaps that is the best confirmation of its authenticity, for no fraudster would set out with such an unlikely story in the hope that he could persuade others to believe it.

Against that of course, we have the big lie theory, much beloved of Adolf Hitler, which maintains that the bigger the lie, the easier it is to convince people to believe it, and he would seem to have had a certain success in that direction. The only difference is that his lie did not last more than twelve years before it was exposed to the world for the evil that it was, but the Christian claim of Christ's resurrection has survived over twenty centuries, and no matter how often it has been attacked and how effectively it has been explained away, it still survives and still demands the full-hearted acceptance of people from the most diverse corners of life.

What, then, is this resurrection which Christians celebrate on Easter Sunday? Who exactly rose from the dead? Did he have any help? What significance did it have for those who first heard of it? What kind of evidence do we have that it ever happened? Are the 'witnesses' reliable sources? Can their different accounts of the events be reconciled or are we left with a confused jumble of facts and fairy tales?

Let us go back to the start, to where the very idea of resurrection originated, and see if, as some have claimed, the pious expectations of a few uncritical believers have given rise to an event which confirms and completes the wishful thinking of many.

In the history of the Jewish people and their relationship with God as recorded in the Bible, we do not find any clear idea of rising from death to a new kind of life until quite late on – that is, no mention of it is made by such central figures as Adam or Abraham or Moses or even David or Solomon; but about seven hundred years before the coming of Christ, we have the prophet Isaiah saying, 'Your dead will come to life, their corpses will rise'; and about two hundred years later, we have Job saying, 'After my awaking, he will set me close to him, and from my flesh I will look on God'; and then, about a hundred and sixty years before the coming of Christ, we have prophet Daniel writing, 'Of those who lie sleeping in the dust of the earth many will awake, some to everlasting life, some to shame and everlasting disgrace'.

From these excerpts, we gather that there was a certain expectation of rising to a new and enjoyable life, mostly geared to those who lived good lives, for there is the suggestion, running parallel to these extracts, that those who do not behave well on earth will suffer punishment by being deprived of the chance to enter into this new life. Some experts have suggested that the biblical idea of resurrection was borrowed from other civilisations, for example the Persians, but there is very little evidence to support any of them. The Jewish people firmly believed, out of their long contact with a God who was always faithful to them and in whom they had always put their trust, that He would not allow the evil man to get away scot free nor the just man to lose his reward.

This same theme of heavenly reward for the righteous is taken up by Jesus in his preaching. 'If your eye should cause you to sin, tear it out; it is better for you to enter the Kingdom of God with one eye than to have two eyes and be thrown into hell'. He also talks about the foreigners who will come from the East and the West to take their places with Abraham, Isaac and Jacob at the feast in the Kingdom of Heaven, and he tells the sick and the suffering to 'rejoice when that day comes and dance for joy, for your reward will be great in Heaven'. These are the ideas of resurrection that would have been reasonably familiar to the Jewish people at the time that interests us. Jesus, however, takes the current idea of resurrection a step further because he has to answer the Sadducees – a group who by family tradition served as priests in the Temple, but who had learned down the years to modify their more extreme traditions and to work out a reasonable compromise with their Roman conquerors.

Jesus had to deal with them because they preached that there was no resurrection, and to make their point they presented him with an outrageously unlikely, but theoretically possible, case of a woman having outlived her seven husbands, and now they demanded to know, 'Whose wife will she be at the resurrection?' And Jesus has to point out to them that they will not rise to the old life they lived here on earth, but to a new transformed style of life where the power of God will be displayed in ways unimaginable to mere mortals.

Jesus makes three predictions of his own resurrection, according to the gospel of St Mark, but they are all a bit too cut and dried to be accepted as the actual words of Jesus himself. 'The Son of Man will be delivered into the hands of men; they will put him to death; and three days after he has been put to death he will rise again'. This sounds more like the cool clinical statement of a well-meaning biographer who would have wanted Jesus to say something along these lines in order to prepare his followers for what was to come. Nonetheless, it fits into that theme of resurrection where the just man will have to endure suffering and even persecution if he is to live out to the full his religious beliefs, but where he will undoubtedly be vindicated by God who is always faithful to those who put their lives into his hands.

We can see that the idea of resurrection after death was not a novel idea to the Jewish people at the time of Jesus, but neither was it a firmly based conviction and expectation in the heart of every member of the community. The Sadducees rejected the idea outright, and there were undoubtedly many others who held no strong opinion on the matter, one way or the other. It cannot be argued that Jesus had overcome the doubts of his followers on the matter by preparing them psychologically and emotionally for this unlikely event. In nearly every instance where Jesus mentions his resurrection, the writers of the sacred books are at pains to point out that the reaction of his followers to this news was either confusion or disbelief: 'But they did not understand what he said and were afraid to ask him'. And Peter, his right-hand man, found the idea that Jesus would be crucified and rise again so repugnant that he tried, in very human fashion, to persuade his beloved leader not to talk in such a negative fashion.

The utterly disgraceful way in which Jesus was about to die produced a reaction that was more discouraging than his followers' lack of mental preparation. Whatever chance there was of a charismatic and respected leader of the people persuading them to believe in his forthcoming resurrection from the dead, there was no chance that a convicted criminal, put to death on a cross, would be able to do it, for in the eyes of the Jewish community, from the days of Moses right down to the scribes of Qumran, a man who met death by crucifixion was already cursed and abandoned by God. A crucified messiah or saviour was a contradiction in terms – as St Paul put it, 'an obstacle to the Jews' –

and a crucified messiah who had risen from the dead was a joke in extremely bad taste.

The people who opposed Jesus while he was still alive, the civil and religious authorities who regarded him as a dangerous rabble-rouser, and not a few of the ordinary people who saw him as a well-meaning but troublesome critic of the traditions of their race, looked around for some way to undermine this burgeoning belief in his resurrection, and they focused their attention on an interpretation that would hopefully drive a wedge into the mass of convinced believers, rather than meet them with a head-on denial. They suggested that the resurrection of Jesus was a figurative rather than a factual event, that it was merely a symbolic description of the way in which the spirit and teachings of Jesus had survived his death and were now animating the hearts and minds of his followers. But there was nothing in the reports of his disciples that could be bent around to this way of thinking. The very language and the idioms of St Paul, for example, when he uses phrases like 'Jesus Christ and God the Father who raised him from the dead', clearly indicate that he is referring to something factual that happened to Jesus after his death and not to some psychological incentive in the minds of his followers.

From all this, we may reasonably conclude that the followers of Jesus, while accepting the theoretical possibility of rising from the dead at the end of time, had no concrete reason to expect the resurrection of Jesus other than the warnings he had given them himself, and as we have seen, their reaction to these was disbelief. In face of such a negative attitude, what evidence can we present that would explain the apostles' subsequent U-turn from utter disbelief to a firm conviction that Jesus had in fact risen from the dead. (The one thing that we do not have is an eyewitness to the resurrection. No one saw him rise from the dead, and this gap in the evidence for the resurrection annoyed some early Christians, so much that they even invented an Apocryphal Gospel of St Peter in the second century, complete with eyewitnesses, to fill the gap, but it never gained any credence among genuine Christians.)

The answer to the question, 'Why did the apostles believe in the resurrection?' is the simplest of all answers. They believed Jesus had risen from the dead because they met him and talked with him after he had risen from the dead. Admittedly, they were not immediately convinced, and some, like Thomas, were not easily convinced, but the basic reason why the disciples and the other close followers of Jesus could go out and proclaim his resurrection was that they had actually met him and spoken with him after the event. The fact that his tomb was empty on Easter Sunday morning – a fact that even his enemies did not dispute – was a pointer to his resurrection; but, as his enemies were quick to point out, the tomb could have been empty because, as they subsequently tried to make out, the apostles had come secretly during the night and stolen it away. In any case, it did not persuade the followers of Jesus that he had risen from the dead, because their first conclusion was, like that of Mary Magdalen, that someone else had come during the night and made off with the body. It was only when they later met the risen Jesus that they made the connection between the empty tomb and his resurrection.

The various meetings of the risen Jesus with his followers still leaves us with the vital question, 'Is the evidence of these people reliable?' There are good reasons for thinking so, not least of which is the unsuitability of the very first witnesses and the subsequent down-to-earth way in which the whole business was reported.

All accounts agree that Christ first appeared to some women, which points to some very bad planning on the part of anyone trying to fabricate a convincing story about a resurrection, for in those pre-feminist days, a woman did not count as a reliable witness in any matter under investigation, an attitude borne out by the apostles themselves when they dismissed the women's report of the resurrection as nonsense and refused to believe it. The ideal witness would have been one of the senior apostles, as they were most likely to carry some weight in the prevailing cultural and religious atmosphere. The other convincing argument is the very matter-of-fact and unadorned way in which the appearances of Jesus to his apostles and followers were reported.

In other instances in the Scriptures where God makes contact with people, the setting is usually one of dreams or ecstasies, or the darkness of night or the blinding vision of the transfiguration, but in the reports of the resurrection it is a very clinical unadorned statement of fact. 'He showed himself to the eleven themselves while they were at table. He reproached them for their incredulity and obstinacy because they refused to believe those who had seen him after he had risen'. Or again, 'Jesus came and stood among them. He said, 'Peace be with you', and showed them his hands and his side'. It was as though the facts themselves were so indisputable and so compelling that no emphasis or poetic exaggeration was necessary to persuade people to believe him.

The air of quiet confidence on the part of the sacred writers is understandable, and yet the absence of a more majestic and a more authoritative proclamation of the resurrection of Jesus Christ is surprising because it was on the evidence of these few witnesses that the church of Christ was to be built. They alone did not have to rely on the dependability of someone else's report; they alone were moved by experience and not by faith. They are set aside from others in St John's famous distinction between those who have seen and believed and those who have not seen and yet believed, and in St Paul's brief account of the post-resurrection history of the Church, 'I taught you (…) that Christ was buried and that he was raised to life on the third day, in accordance with the Scriptures; that he appeared first to Cephas and secondly to the Twelve. Next, he appeared to more than five hundred of the brothers at the same time, most of whom are still alive, though some have died. Then he appeared to James and then to all the apostles; and last of all he appeared to me too; it was as though I had been born when no one expected it'. They are a group apart, never to be repeated, who have met and spoken with Christ after his resurrection. For that was the great thrust of Christianity, driven home by the resurrection, that Jesus was the Son of God as he had claimed, and now this claim was substantiated by his rising from the dead. Others, like Lazarus, had been raised from the dead, but Jesus had boldly and accurately foretold his own resurrection – as the apostles began to remember – and that put him way above the level of mortal man and on a par with the God of life and death.

Nowadays we tend to look upon the resurrection as the final revelation of Jesus to us as the Son of God rather than as a proof of his divinity. From a helpless baby, he had grown and revealed himself through his preaching and miracles as the Son of God sent to bring the good news of a God who is a loving father to his people, and to win forgiveness for their sins by his death and resurrection. He has not just made a brief appearance in court as it were, on our behalf, but he has become one of us, sharing our suffering and leading us now through death into the everlasting life of Heaven.

Of course all our historical research and logical arguments are worthless if we do not have faith. I can lay all the facts of Jesus' life, death and resurrection before one man and he says, 'My Lord and my God'. I can lay the same facts before another man and he will say, 'My God, you don't expect me to believe that'. We have to believe without having seen; in other words, we need to have faith, and faith is the gift of God, for not all the learning of the learned, nor the wisdom of the wise will bring us an inch nearer to God until we can say, with the father of the epileptic child, 'I do have faith. Help the little faith that I have'.

Cartoons by
Joe Connolly

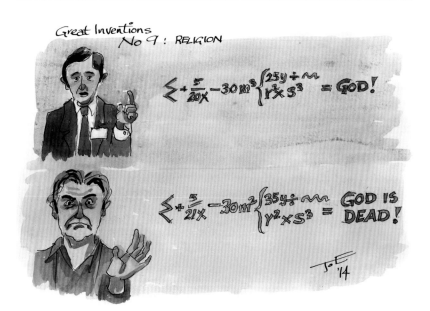

Seanfhocla
IRISH PROVERBS

Tús maith leath na hoibre   A GOOD START IS HALF THE WORK

Seanfhocla
IRISH PROVERBS

An rud is anam is iontach
WHAT IS RARE IS WONDERFUL

Ġearann beirt bóchar
COMPANY SHORTENS THE ROAD

Is fearr rith maich ná droch sheasamh
BETTER TO RUN THAN MAKE A BAD STAND

IRISH LIFE –
"Transvestite"

Articles

Chapel Road Bomb

It was a normal morning in Waterside Parochial House until the impact of the explosion lifted us off our feet and the unmerciful bang left our ears tingling. It came from the direction of the hill behind us, an area where most of the domestic staff lived, and where one of our own colleagues had recently moved, so everyone ran screaming in the direction of the explosion, desperately calling out the names of their loved ones and praying that their lives had been spared.

None of us knew what kind of bomb had gone off, nor even where precisely it had happened, but even had we known it would have made no difference whatever to our reaction. The warning of the bomb disposal officer, solemnly delivered to us in a lecture at the outset of the Troubles, 'If you can see the device, it can kill you', made no impact. At the time, it sounded a bit melodramatic, and it took another incident some years later to convince us that there might be some truth in what he had said. A young man of revolutionary inclinations had planted a bomb in a busy bus station and then retired to what he considered a safe distance to observe his handiwork. The explosion lobbed many large concrete blocks into the air – one of them landed with unerring accuracy on the head of the young revolutionary, with fatal results.

But that lay in the past. For the present we ran into the danger zone as hard as we could, some to discover the fate of family and loved ones, some to go to the help of the injured and frightened, and some because it was our job to attend the wounded and the dying with the prayers and sacraments of the Church.

I was young and energetic and arrived first at the scene of the explosion, a car bomb that had detonated when the driver turned the key to start his engine. The victim was a familiar neighbour to all of us, a true-blue supporter of all things republican who made no bones about his allegiance, and for that reason, it would appear, he had come to the attention of some of the opposing patriots.

He was still alive, and breathing very hoarsely. His upper body was intact, but his legs were a dreadful sight, massively swollen and seeping blood from hundreds of shrapnel wounds. I could do absolutely nothing for his physical comfort. I knew nothing about first aid, but I had the distinct impression that if I tried to move him, I could do irreparable harm, so I stuck to what I knew and gave him the last rites of the Church, praying that he might recover from his wounds, but acknowledging the gravity of the situation and asking God to forgive his sins, and if he were to die, to welcome him into his eternal home in Heaven.

At that point the army bomb squad arrived and an officer with an upper-class accent took me gently but firmly by the arm and said, 'If you will come with me, Padre. I think we should retire to a safer distance'. I was tempted to tell him that it was my job to work from unsafe distances, and it would have been genuinely and sincerely meant, for in those early days of my priesthood, it was understood that if you had to walk through a minefield to get to the dying, you started walking. It was not heroic. It was your job. However, by this time, I had completed the essentials of my job and I did not want to get into an argument with the well-spoken officer, so I accompanied him in silence to the perimeter he had set up around the incident.

'You realise, Padre, that if you can see the device it can kill you', he began as soon as we hunkered down behind his jeep. I was tempted to tell him that it was my job to take these risks, just like himself, but I doubt if he would have considered his duty to obey orders and risk his life in battle on the same plane as the anointing with oil and the pious incantations of some innocent clergyman.

It took us some time to get things organised, but the victim was eventually taken off to the hospital, where he lost both legs but where they saved his life.

As the officer and myself packed up our belongings, I said to him, 'I inherited a diary that a clerical colleague kept during his time as chaplain to the British Army in the First World War. He was very emphatic that a chaplain was not a holy man who sat behind the lines and prayed for the success of the troops up at the front – at least not in his Church. He was judged by how willing he was to creep into no-man's land and give the last rites to a dying soldier. It did not change the tactical situation at the front in any way, but it radically affected the faith and the belief of those who were about to go into battle. And, believe it or not, that is how we still think'.

Today, fifty years later, it has not changed; but the bureaucrats have taken over and now, we are rarely allowed near scenes of death or destruction. The fire brigade, the ambulance, the doctors, the forensic teams, the police and the social services will all be allowed to enter the scene of a crime or an accident, while the priest stands patiently in the wings, waiting to be allowed to administer the last rites, and only in the most exceptional circumstances will he be allowed anywhere near the victim. Even then, he will be expected to give a sample of DNA as well as blood details and fingerprints before he departs, but by that time the victim is usually dead.

Baptismal Fonts

The baptismal fonts in our new and renovated churches tend to reflect the ambiguity of the Church's thinking on Baptism. Floating around in the recesses of its conscious mind is the suspicion, if not the conviction, that immersion is the only logical and historical way of Baptism; but the obvious difficulties of submerging an adult without flooding the basement, and the no less obvious difficulties of attiring the naked form, male or female, in some suitably asexual and opaque garment for the occasion, must have proved too much for the sheltered souls of the early episcopate, for they settled for the best compromise available – what might be called the devotional equivalent of a quick splash around the ears and neck while leaning over the kitchen sink.

It did little for the dramatic soul of the liturgy professor, but it satisfied the expectations of the ecclesiastical lawyer, for as in the days of your childhood, when your mother asked you if you had washed your face, you could always answer truthfully that you had, even though the quick rub with a damp flannel that you had just administered was a long way from the cleansing bath that your mother had classified as the minimum essential. Today's trickle of water down the forehead of the baptismal candidate hardly requires a font four feet plus in diameter, but you are going to have some difficulty immersing an adult in it, unless he hangs his legs over the side, though some provision for adults will have to be made if immersion of infants ever becomes the norm.

That, however, is unlikely to happen, if only because of the danger of civil suits against any clergyman unlucky enough to

a) drop the child into the water, b) hold it under for too long, c) expose it to chills and pneumonia by using water that is too cold, or d) endanger its health through risk of contagion by immersing it in the water that Joe Soap's pimply child has just vacated.

We finish up, therefore, with a compromise: a font that is too small for immersion, but big enough to collect all the water that will ever be poured on the foreheads of all the infants of the parish for a century to come. We find the same compromise in new or renovated houses. Instead of throwing out the bath – an inadequate and antiquated method of washing – and substituting in its place the shower, we regularly find the shower positioned over the bath, so that when we slip – as we are always likely to do – we land on our heads because there is nothing to hold on to. For some inexplicable reason, we feel duty-bound to hold fast to the drawbacks of the old system when we introduce the advantages of the new. There is a kind of guilt about abandoning the difficulties of the past.

If, as seems likely, Baptism will be carried out for the foreseeable future by pouring water over the forehead of the candidate, it seems reasonable to assume that baptismal fonts will only need to be big enough to collect and dispose of the drainage. Anything bigger is merely another indication of our reluctance to leave the past behind and our pathological fear of embracing any form of change.

Ecumenical Talk – Macosquin

Let me say at the outset that if you were hoping for some kind of intellectual explanation of the fundamentals of your faith and mine, and a possible reconciliation of their differences, then I am afraid you will be disappointed. I am not an intellectual. I have no expertise in matters of theology or philosophy, and in some ways that is an advantage, because religion is not about intelligence. It is about faith. I can be the brightest man in the world and still have no belief, and I can be the humblest person on earth and have faith that will move mountains.

Believe it or not, I started my clerical life in this parish fifty-four years ago. I lived at the top of Captain Street in Coleraine, attached to St John's Church. And my earliest memory of ministry is hearing confessions in that church on a Saturday night while a clergyman of another denomination – who will remain nameless – stood at the gate with a loudspeaker and, in as loud a voice as possible, informed my parishioners that only God could forgive sins, a sentiment with which I found myself in complete agreement. Even though the words that I spoke to every penitent were, 'May God give you pardon and peace', and the nearest I came to independent action was when I said in conclusion, 'I absolve you in the name of the Father and of the Son and of the Holy Spirit', my clerical colleague still continued to denounce me. The possibility that the Father and the Son and the Holy Spirit might not always agree with me had already occurred to me, and left me in no doubt that, whatever about passing on the message, matters of forgiveness were firmly in the hands of God. But that was the state of inter-

Church dialogue in those days, and most of us had little enough notion of what we believed ourselves, and much less notion about what others believed.

On the Catholic side, we all believed in the importance of rules and regulations. If the bishop said Catholics were not allowed to attend services in Protestant churches, we toed the line and finished up with the kind of absurdity recalled by Dean Victor Griffin, when members of the Dublin government, ministers of state, skulked around the precincts of Christ Church Cathedral in Dublin, trying to look inconspicuous, while the funeral service of the president of their country was taking place inside. Some years later, a Catholic president, Mary McAleese, was attacked from numerous quarters for having received Holy Communion in an Anglican church. The subsequent argument about the presence of Christ in Holy Communion was more notable for its intellectual arrogance than for its humble acceptance of truth.

Many years later, during my time in Limavady, we had a kind of mutual pastoral visitation where we visited each church in turn, and the minister would explain the basic beliefs of their particular church and the nature of their service. Everyone believed in the presence of Christ in their communion services. It was only when someone started trying to explain the nature of that presence that we had problems, and the Catholic Church was the biggest offender, because we had a theory called 'transubstantiation', based on Greek philosophy, which was seen as an explanation, whereas in fact, it was merely a substitution of new words for old. In practice, as I'm sure you know, the main difference is that we believe that Christ continues to be present in the Holy Communion and hence can be brought by lay ministers to the sick and infirm and those who are unable to attend church services.

At this point, I must apologise unashamedly for stealing from a learned friend and colleague of mine who died recently, and who spoke eloquently on the subject of inter-Church relationships many years ago at a similar service in St Mary's, Limavady. He was three times as smart as the rest of us and he homed in without hesitation on the fundamental cause of religious quarrelling and bickering. He quoted from the prophet Zachariah: 'In those days, ten men from all languages and nations will take hold of one Jew by the sleeve of his robe and say, 'Let us go with you because we have heard that God is with you". In our own day, how many lost souls have taken any of us by the sleeve of our robe and asked, 'Can I go with you because I have heard that God is with you?' And there may lie the answer to our religious divisions.

If the followers of Christ are growing fewer every day, it is because they no longer feel inclined to reach for the sleeve of our robes and follow us. Without any doubt, we have not provided the kind of leadership that is called for. At one point, however, I disagreed with my friend. He said, 'It is not enough simply to bring people of opposing views together just to talk. They may get to know each other and even get on well together, but few are likely to confront each other about any subject they feel strongly about, so the prejudice separating them remains unaddressed'. I would contend that the starting point for dialogue is to get to know one another. It is always easier to argue with a friend than with a stranger. I base this on my own experience of life, of growing up in a mixed community where we inevitably encountered people of a different faith and culture. My father was a cattle dealer/farmer, and he bought and sold with everyone, and everyone bought and sold with him, which meant that our good Presbyterian neighbour was liable to wander in as we were reciting our evening Rosary, but it didn't worry him, or us, in the least. He simply sat down and waited until the prayers were finished, and even joined in the occasional 'Our Father' without a qualm. Because we were friends, we could handle any situation without anxiety.

I remember telling a friend from a different background that evening prayers in our house consisted of the Rosary, followed by prayers and petitions for everyone in need, and it was always a long list, all recited at breakneck speed by my father, who was probably afraid of losing his rhythm and forgetting his lines if he slowed down, only to be told that I had confirmed a long-standing belief among Protestants that Catholics galloped through their prayers at breakneck speed and never paused to meditate or to consider the meaning of what they were saying. He was right. That was our style, that was our culture. But then, if your education finished at thirteen, maybe that is why you did not concentrate on meaning and why you were content to have given God and God alone that time of prayer.

Let me finish with a few fundamental principles. We can only learn from those who are different from us. We cannot learn from people who think exactly the same as ourselves. We also have to remind ourselves that we have more in common than we realise. We should cherish what we have in common and cherish equally what makes us different. It will be a sign that we have moved on a step if we can recognise that we have hurt each other very badly in the past, and that none of us can call ourselves innocent until we make a real effort to confront the truth for ourselves and for others. At the same time, it is beyond question that we have also enriched each other over the years. There is no hard and fast rule for coping with difference. Sometimes it calls for patience, sometimes it calls for directness and sometimes it calls for humour.

True Healing

The role and focus of the priest in any crisis situation is obviously misunderstood by most of today's medical profession. In the context of terminal illness, they treat us as people of marginal ability and no importance.

At the very best, our role is seen as consoler of the bereaved and intermediary between the family and officialdom. We are good at persuading the family that there has to be a post mortem, for example, but we are kept well back from the patient as long as he has life in him. Doctors and paramedics regularly leave us standing in the corridors, or sitting on the stairs, while they tidy up the patient and make him presentable. Dead, but presentable.

We must get the message through to the medical profession that we do not operate on dead people, any more than they do. We are a sacramental church. We use the signs and symbols of the Christian faith, which we call sacraments, to put the power of God to work on the sick and the dying. When they are dead, we will certainly pray for them, but while they are alive, we confer the sacrament of the sick upon them and give them the Eucharist, in the firm belief that the power of God acts through these sacraments. Our role is to influence the outcome of events, not just to pick up the pieces once the medical team has departed.

Our role is as real and as physical as that of the medics. We are there not just to offer some consoling prayers after the event, but to influence the outcome of the event for good, just as effectively as a doctor giving an injection or as a nurse providing oxygen. We confer sacraments which have a real and rational purpose. We cannot prophesy that immediate healing will result from the sacrament of the sick, nor that bodily strength will result from the reception of the Eucharist, but neither can a doctor guarantee the effects of an injection nor a nurse the benefits of a procedure. They administer the remedies and hope that nature will combine with their efforts and produce a positive result. We too administer our remedies in the same way and hope that they will work.

There is no more sense to leaving the priest out in the corridor until the patient is dead, expecting him to work some long-distance magic, than there is to admitting the doctor only after the patient has died. His injections are not meant for dead people. Neither are our sacraments.

Religious Programmes

I often wonder, can a non-religious person, your average home-grown atheist, humanist or basic unbeliever, produce a successful religious programme. Pasolini, with his Gospel of St Matthew, would seem to have answered that question. But not every producer is a Pasolini. Cecil B. DeMille used to drag a few dancing girls into his pictures when the action slowed down. And one gets glimpses of a similar if smaller-scale tactic on the part of hard-pressed TV producers when the ratings begin to lag.

For myself, I would like them to create religious programmes where the congregation is as ordinary as you will find in your church on a Sunday morning. I am not likely to get dancing girls leading the entrance procession, though God knows nowadays anything is possible. But neither do I want cancer victims reading the lessons, handicapped children bringing up the gifts, conservationists or animal lovers doing the prayers of the faithful unless these people are an integral and regular part of the congregation. Instead, I want the shopkeepers, the tax inspectors, the farmers, the factory workers and all the other ordinary people who make up any congregation on a Sunday morning doing the same things on the TV screen. Religion is not a pastime for the marginalised. In fact, I have always found that the people on the margins tend to be far more committed to their faith than the rest of us, and in far less need of our patronising privileges. Religion is a formative drive and a central responsibility in everyone's life. And the sooner we stop apologising for it by trying to make it into an entertainment the better. If you believe in God, you have to worship God. That is my firm and rooted opinion. There is no way around it. If you believe that your life is ultimately and completely dependent on God, if you believe that the air you breathe and the ground you walk on are his creation, then you have no choice but to get down on your knees and worship Him. Of course you can neglect God and forget God and disregard God because you are thoroughly enjoying yourself doing other things. And that I can understand, though I won't necessarily agree with it. But what you cannot do is claim to believe in God and do nothing about it without being a hypocrite. For Catholics like myself, this worship takes the form of prayer and the Mass, and especially the Mass. And if we neglect it, we cannot truthfully claim to believe in God. Worship, as I have said before, is work, hard work, in which you have to be personally involved. If you treat it as the religious equivalent of a rock concert, you are going to be bored out of your mind. For worship does not set out to entertain you. If anything, worship is your attempt to entertain God. And the ultimate question to be asked is not how much you enjoy God's contribution, but rather how much did God enjoy your own feeble efforts.

The Fear of Fallibility

It is hard to believe that such a warm and caring expression as 'Feed my lambs, feed my sheep' could be taken for anything but a truly pastoral concern for the weak and the vulnerable. And yet for centuries it has been at the heart of the Catholic Church's claim to exercise authority over its members in the name of Christ. In fact, so concerned were we about power and authority that in the last century, we declared the pope to be infallible, in the rather naive hope that, if a pope has authority, then an infallible pope will have even more authority.

This, of course, can be misconstrued as an attack on a traditional doctrine of the Church, but my purpose is merely to point out that the Church's endless concern with authority and power makes no sense at a time when the rest of the world is talking about leadership and community.

Infallibility is not an implausible doctrine. It is merely an impossible one, but no more untrue, for that reason, than a trip to Mars is untrue because at present it is impossible. Within the limits of human language, it is not possible to set a dogma of the faith and say, 'Henceforth and for ever this is the truth, unchanging and unchangeable, immune to the tides of fashion and the winds of change, constant and invariable to the end of time'. And it is not possible because everything on this earth is in a constant process of change, including the very words we speak. We grow up and we grow old. We ripen and we wither. We grow fat and we grow thin. We learn and we forget. We never stand still. And the words that we speak lose their shape and their focus even when we try to freeze them in the arid definitions and doctrines of the faith. They mean something different every time we look at them. And that is why Christ did not depend on dogmas or definitions to create his church. They were too stiff, too unyielding. Instead he chose stories that would bend to the shape of every generation, and persuasion that answered the deepest needs of every soul.

The experts in the management business have in our own day rediscovered the importance of leading the workforce rather than driving it. But they are merely putting into action what Christ said two thousand years ago. 'I have come not to be served, but to serve and to give life as a ransom for many'. Leadership in his eyes meant harnessing and guiding the gifts of others, and forgetting about his own position and power. It was when he gave up everything and seemed to lose everything on the Cross that he gained his true victory and began to renew the face of the earth.

The Right Reasons

My first parish priest, back in 1960, told me that he was once ordered by his bishop to publicly excommunicate one of his parishioners. I cannot remember what the offence was – back in those days, you could be excommunicated for blowing your nose at the wrong time – but it was a technical offence, like marrying outside the Catholic Church, rather than a straightforward sin, like beating up your wife, and the parish priest was anything but enthusiastic about carrying out the sentence. He knew from the hard road of experience that while the bishop might see this as an individual and personal offence, the victim's family might take an entirely different view; and, sure enough, when the time came and Joe Bloggs heard himself duly expelled with all solemnity from the Church of his youth, and his neighbours warned to have nothing further to do with him, the sentence worked better than anyone could have anticipated, because not only did Joe stay away from the Church, but his brothers and his sisters and his cousins and his aunts all stayed away in sympathy and never darkened its door again.

It was a very understandable reaction, and yet, it was not a good enough reason for leaving the Church. It was a good enough reason for raising hell about the cruelty and the insensitivity and the stupidity of the Church's leaders and the Church's procedures, but the only good enough reason for leaving the Church is because you think its teaching is false. If you do not believe that Jesus is the Son of God – and you can spend most of a lifetime of study, trying to justify such a stance – then you can reject the Church, but not because you are feeling sore at it. In thirty-two years of priesthood, I have heard parishioners presenting every conceivable excuse for leaving the Church, from the size of the curate's car to the dropping of the Latin Mass, but never have I heard a logical or a rational answer given before someone packed his bags and renounced his allegiance to the Church of his birth. The same people who would shortlist you for the funny farm if you suggested that they abandon the family car because it had a flat tyre, or who would urge you to leave the home of your childhood because it needed a coat of paint, still seem congenitally incapable of transferring this same kind of wisdom to their faith. If the car has no engine or the house has no roof, you might reasonably abandon them both, but if the car has a dented mudguard or the house has a broken window, it makes little sense to walk away from them. If we can do nothing better, we live with the defects, and if we can do something better, we put things right.

If Joe Bloggs had written to the bishop who ordered his excommunication and asked how the Church could justify humiliating him before the entire assembly, for doing something which a short time previously had been a perfectly acceptable practice in the eyes of the Church, he might have stopped the procedure in its tracks. If it was perfectly right and reasonable in 1899 for him to marry his Anglican fiancée in the Church to which she belonged, why was it such a heinous crime in 1959 to do the same? Obedience was such a respected virtue that even when bishops found themselves confronting unreasonable demands, they tended to toe the ecclesiastical line.

Sincerity was another so-called virtue which often led people into making the most catastrophic decisions. As long as you were sincere, you were seen as making the right decision. The possibility that you might be sincerely wrong never seemed to occur to anyone. When the Duchess of Kent joined the Catholic Church some years ago, many broadminded members of the Anglican faith expressed the opinion that there could be no objection to the move, as long as she was sincere. Rumour had it that she had changed churches because the Anglican Church was now ordaining women, but I sincerely hope that is not true, because there is no guarantee that the Catholic Church will not do the same at some date in the future. I shall not be around when it happens, but I am quite confident that the day will come when, not merely will the Catholic clergy be allowed to marry, but women will be admitted to equal status in all aspects of the life of the Catholic Church.

Dot not remind me of all the theological difficulties. If every human instinct in us says, 'This is right', no amount of theological objections will stop us.

Patriots All

I am not a heroic type of person. If anything I am a cowardly person, extremely wary about putting my head above the parapet. I have no ambition whatever to be a hero in battle, or to be proclaimed one of the saviours of the nation. If I must be involved in the community, I just want to get home again as quickly as possible, with the least possible damage done to my body, my spirit or my standing in the community.

There was a time when I might have been self-conscious about my cowardice, but not any more. I have learned that we all start out in life with a limited ration of courage in our knapsacks, and every time we encounter the enemy, we use up a precious fragment, until the day comes when the supply runs out and we abandon our weapons and run for the hills. We do not care how bad it looks to the passing spectator. We have no concern for the culture of the times or the traditions of the past. We just want to survive whatever battle is being fought, and if some well-meaning but misguided sons of the soil raise the cry 'For God and Ulster' or 'A nation once again', we politely but firmly tell them to take themselves and their futile slogans and consign them forthwith to the disposal bin of history, while we, in the meantime, try to maintain some kind of rational equilibrium between those who think it is all right to take their own lives and those who think it right and reasonable to take the lives of others.

We live in a scary world. For the past fifty years, we have had to contend with the paramilitaries and the crime bosses and the drug dealers and the crackpot politicians. When they were not endangering our lives, they were hindering us from going where we wanted to go and doing what we wanted to do and, sadly, like myself, most people did not have the courage to stand up and say, 'Enough', so the hoodlums were allowed to continue on their demented way. And we have not merely had to live with their particular standards of behaviour, we have had to endure their particular brand of 'culture'; and we are now being persuaded that we should shape our lives around their particular vision of the future.

Remember the gangster film which ended with the cry, 'Is this the end of Rico?' I can only ask, 'Is this the end of Ulster?' while echoing sincerely the heartfelt words of Ted Heath after his first visit to Ulster: 'What a bloody awful country!'

Scripts

Final Stage of the Enquiry into the Death of Oswald Birtwhistle

Centre stage is a small raised platform on which sits a table with a chair behind it. Stage left is another small raised platform with a chair at an angle to the audience.

The Commissioner enters stage right and takes his seat behind the table.

Commissioner: Good morning, ladies and gentlemen. This enquiry is now in its final session. Once again, let me introduce myself. I am Peter Jackson, former High Court judge, now retired, and I have been commissioned by Her Majesty's Government to conduct an enquiry into the death on the fourteenth of October 1998 of Oswald William Birtwhistle as he was travelling along the road between Belfast and Derry.

This enquiry will, it is hoped, shed some light on the wisdom or otherwise of introducing what is called a 'Good Samaritan Law', such as exists at present in some states in America, into the government's legislative programme for next year.

I should point out that this enquiry is not a court of law, and consequently, it does not pass judgment on the words or actions of any of those who have been called to give evidence. It will be left to the conscience of each individual to determine whether they have anything with which to reproach themselves.

Our task is not to determine who killed Oswald Birtwhistle. It is reasonably established by now that he was the victim of a random attack by a gang of criminals who have been responsible for several other attacks in the locality in recent weeks. So far, regretfully, they have not been apprehended.

Our task is to determine, rather, why he was allowed to bleed to death on a public road while other citizens travelled to and fro past him and offered no assistance. This morning we hear the evidence of the final three witnesses in this enquiry

I call the first witness, Reverend George Fulton.

George Fulton enters stage left and takes his seat in the empty chair.
He is a somewhat nervous individual, fingering his collar and speaking rather rapidly.

Please be seated, Reverend Fulton. You understand, Reverend, that while you are not under oath it is expected that you will answer all questions as fully and as accurately as you can.

Fulton: Yes, Your Honour.

Commissioner: Reverend Fulton, the police report tells us that you passed the spot where Mr Birtwhistle was lying at approximately half past nine on Sunday morning. Can you tell us, what did you see or do on that occasion?

Fulton: I was already late, you know. I had a service in Bandon Church at ten o'clock and I was already way behind time, and I had a lot of things on my mind because the verger in Bandon is off sick and I had to be there early to open the church and to turn on the heating and so on. My mind was not really on the road, and I was very nearly past the body before it struck me that it might in fact be a body. All I could see was legs sticking out into the road.

                      I thought about going back to investigate, but I was so pushed for time, and to be quite truthful, I thought to myself, 'It's not the first time that I've seen a man sleeping off the effects of a Saturday night drinking binge by the roadside on a Sunday morning'.

Commissioner: So you passed him by?

Fulton: Well, I suppose I did – if you insist on putting it like that.

Commissioner: Oh, I do, I do, Reverend Fulton.
                      You mentioned that you were on your way to conduct a religious service that morning. It occurs to me that, like myself, some of

your listeners here may wonder how you intended reconciling the Christian message of compassion and care with your summary disregard of Mr Birtwhistle's distress. Could one say that Christ would have given priority to punctuality and good order over concern for the wounds of a dying man?

Fulton: No. One could not. Christ would have always put people first. I can assure Your Honour that I make no attempt to defend my behaviour on this occasion.

In this instance I allowed the pressures of life and duty to take priority over my real responsibilities, and I consequently failed a dying man. It is a failure I will have to live with for the rest of my life.

Commissioner: Indeed you will, Reverend Fulton. You may step down.

Call the next witness, Dr Edward Bramley.

Dr Bramley approaches from stage left as Fulton leaves. His attitude is aggressive, his tone guilty.

Commissioner: Please be seated Dr Bramley. While you are not under oath, nor are any of the witnesses to this enquiry, you are expected to answer all questions as fully and as accurately as you can. Do you understand?

Bramley: Yes, Your Honour.

Commissioner: Perhaps then we can begin by asking why it took you three weeks to respond to the

	police appeals for witnesses to this death, since we know that you passed that way on the Sunday morning in question?
Bramley:	Because I was out of the country for two weeks, and because I had nothing to tell concerning this incident. As I have already told the police, I saw nothing on that Sunday morning.
Commissioner:	This is most extraordinary, Dr Bramley. The police report and all the other witnesses have testified that the body of Oswald Birtwhistle was protruding onto the road a distance of three to four feet fifteen minutes before you passed that way and fifteen minutes after you passed that way. Are we to assume that in the intervening half hour some person or persons removed the body until you had passed by and then returned it to its former position?
Bramley:	I can only tell you what I know. I saw no body when I passed that spot.
Commissioner:	Most extraordinary. However, let us retrace our steps a little further, Dr Bramley, and see if we can find some reasonable explanation for this strange paradox.
	You say you were on the road at a quarter to ten, but you were not on a duty rota or answering a sick call. May one ask where you were going at that time of morning?
Bramley:	I was going home.

Commissioner:	Home? You were going home at a quarter to ten in the morning. Which leads, I think, to the inevitable question: where were you going home from at this time?
Bramley:	I had been to a function in the Regal Hotel and I stayed the night.
Commissioner:	I see. Was that a professional function? A workshop perhaps, or a lecture by one of your colleagues?
Bramley:	No. It was a social function.
Commissioner:	I see. Was the function in celebration of some event or achievement?
Bramley:	It was to celebrate the fact that one of my colleagues was about to get married.
Commissioner:	Oh, a stag night, as they say. Would that be a correct description, Dr Bramley?
Bramley:	Yes, I suppose so.
Commissioner:	Would it be reasonable, then, to assume, Dr Bramley, that a fair amount of alcohol was consumed at this function, and that perhaps even you had drunk deeply before the night was out?
Bramley:	I did have a few drinks, yes.
Commissioner:	A few drinks, Doctor. We can, if you wish, call the manager of this establishment, who will testify that he served you with seven double whiskeys before exhaustion

eventually overtook him and he went to his bed at two o'clock. May we ask, Doctor, at what time you finally retired to bed? And please remember that your movements can be checked quite easily with the hotel staff, if need be.

Bramley: It must have been after four o'clock.

Commissioner: It was in fact at ten minutes to five that you were carried to your bed by a combination of your colleagues and members of the hotel staff – all of whom, I gather, had good reason to remember your departure.

Bramley: So? I'm entitled to take a drink if I want to. It's nobody's business but mine.

Commissioner: Regretfully, Dr Bramley, there are circumstances where it is indeed other people's business if you take a drink. For instance, it is the business of the police and every other road user if you drink so much that you find yourself driving home after a function – even after a few hours sleep – with an alcohol level that is still drastically above the legal limit. It is also, tragically, the business of the sick and the injured, if you are so intoxicated that you cannot safely carry out your professional duties. I do not say that these circumstances arose in your case, but I ask you once again, what did you see on the road as you drove from Belfast to Derry at a quarter to ten on Sunday morning?

Bramley: *Heatedly.* I tell you, I saw nothing out of the ordinary.

Commissioner:	*Slowly.* Nothing out of the ordinary. And there we must leave it. You may step down.

Call the final witness, Mr Robert Mellon.

Bramley departs and Robert Mellon takes the seat. Slightly pompous.

Commissioner:	Mr Mellon, you are, I understand, a retired teacher, and you give a laudable amount of your time to working as a counsellor for the Samaritans, yet you made no effort to come to the aid of an injured man who was lying by the roadside. Surely this was a God-given opportunity for you to put your beliefs and your principles into practice.
Mellon:	Your Honour, I have learned most of the lessons of life the hard way. I tend to be suspicious in every circumstance and to assume the worst in all cases. If, as has happened recently, an old pensioner in Strangford can be lured into an empty house and then robbed, I thought it only prudent to consider that maybe I was about to be lured into going to the aid of someone who was merely pretending to be injured.
Commissioner:	And so you did not go to this man's assistance?
Mellon:	I did not go to his assistance.
Commissioner:	Purely out of fear that it might be, as they say, a 'set up', and that you might yourself become a victim?
Mellon:	Purely for that reason.

Commissioner:	Even though your passenger could easily have raised the alarm if anything had gone wrong.
Mellon:	*Silence*
Commissioner:	You did not mention your passenger in your statement to the police, Mr Mellon. Why was that?
Mellon:	Well, it just didn't seem fair that she should be caught up in all this publicity on my account. I was merely giving her a lift home.
Commissioner:	Your passenger is a colleague from your voluntary work, is that not so? I see. Is there by any chance a special relationship between you and this colleague?
Mellon:	Certainly not. She is a voluntary helper like myself and gives generously of her spare time to help others.
Commissioner:	Forgive me, Mr Mellon. Like yourself, I have grown old in the ways of the world and have developed a certain suspicion about the motives of those who perform good works. A more cynical person than myself might conclude, for example, that when a man and a woman, who spend a considerable part of their spare time caring for the suffering and the suicidal members of our society, drive past a dying man on a road which leads *away* from their homes without any attempt to give help, one might conclude that they have something to conceal. However, your wife, Mr Mellon, I am sure, will find your account of these events quite convincing.

Mellon: *Silence*

Commissioner: You may stand down.

Ladies and Gentlemen,

It is not my place to comment on the rights
or wrongs of the behaviour of witnesses
before this enquiry. I merely point out that
the Christian Scriptures – to which most of
them would declare some allegiance – tell
of a man who was left dying by the
roadside, but eventually one man came to
his assistance and nursed him back to
health.

Oswald Birtwhistle was not so lucky. It was
his misfortune to encounter in his last
moments men who had reason and law and
common sense on their side and were
content with that and nothing more. Sadly,
he did not need logical and reasonable and
calculating men. He needed a saviour,
someone who would put people before
everything else and he did not get one, and
that is why he died.

The Missing Messiah

*A Report by the Empire Broadcasting Corporation of Judea
into Rumours of the Birth of the Messiah*

PRESENTER: This morning (evening), we take you over to the studios of the Empire Broadcasting Corporation in Jerusalem for a special edition of the *Watchman* programme. Our reporter is Philip of Hebron.

PHILIP: There is a strange tension in the city of Jerusalem today. In the marketplace and on the street corners one can see small groups of men deep in conversation – some voices hushed and respectful, others raised in anger and confusion – but all are discussing the same subject: the possible birth of the long-awaited saviour of the Jewish people, the Messiah. I say 'possible', because while all are agreed that a birth has taken place, not all are agreed about whose birth it has been.

We spoke to Annas, the former high priest of Judaism – one of the most powerful figures in the land.

ANNAS: There is no foundation whatever to the wild rumours that are circulating at present. In fact, they merely belittle the Jewish people and make a mockery of their most sacred beliefs. We have indeed a profound belief that a saviour, a messiah, will come to lead God's people to victory, but he will come with glory and power, a fitting messenger of God the Most High, and not some helpless infant of, to say the least, dubious parentage.

PHILIP: Not everyone would share the high priest's view, but understandably, not everyone is willing to express an opinion publicly. Any deviation from the official teaching can mean exclusion from the temple – and for a Jew that means exclusion from God. However, we did find one person who is so convinced that the Messiah has come that she was willing to risk the wrath of the high priest and the ridicule of the priestly caste. This woman, Anna, the daughter of Phanuel, has no education of any kind, just a profound belief that she would see the Messiah before she died.

ANNA: I know nothing about prophecies or the sacred writings except what I've heard in the synagogue, but God is good. He has promised us a saviour, and he is always true to his promise. The Messiah has come. I can feel it in my bones. I am too old to try and deceive people. He came to the Temple, for the Temple is God's house, the Messiah's house, and that is where I met him. What does it matter that he is still a little baby?

God is with him, and when his time comes
he will have all the power and wisdom he
needs to lead God's people into freedom. I
have waited long years for this privilege,
but now I have seen the Messiah with these
eyes and touched him with these hands, so
I can die in peace.

PHILIP: What has happened to generate such profound and such blind faith?

Our investigations have taken us back to a
most unlikely starting point – the heart of
the empire and the centre of all that is
worldly and un-Jewish – the city of Rome.
Three months ago, the Emperor Augustus
issued a decree that a census was to be
taken of all the peoples of the empire, which
is another way of saying a census of the entire world except for a few barbarous tribes
in the northern reaches of Germany and
Britain. A spokesman from the foreign office
explained the purpose of the census.

F.O. SPOKESMAN: If the empire is to be governed efficiently, it
is essential that we have accurate informa-
tion about the numbers and the location of
the different peoples. If there are a thousand
farmers, for example, cultivating a million
acres in Egypt, we know where to go for
corn when there is a famine in Greece. If
there are twenty thousand skilled horsemen
in Scythia, we know where to recruit an
army to defend our German borders. And it
helps considerably in the matter of equi-
table taxation if we know the profession and
the annual income of all our citizens.

Experience has taught us that the simplest way of getting this information is to ask everyone to return to the home of their own tribe or family. In this way we avoid the duplication and confusion that might otherwise arise. It is merely a practical and simple step towards better government.

PHILIP: A fairly straightforward measure, it might seem, but not to the Jews. To them, census-taking amounts to a challenge to the providence of God. Simon Barabbas, a leading member of the Zealot party.

SIMON: All this talk about better government is sheer rubbish. The census has only one purpose – to make sure that the last drop of tax is squeezed from every citizen and that no one escapes. Once that has been accomplished, everything else falls into place. The emperor can pay his armies to crush anyone who complains. If there is such fair and reasonable government everywhere, why is it necessary to keep a full-strength garrison in Judah all the time?

PHILIP: Whatever the true reason behind it, the census went ahead as planned, and among the millions temporarily uprooted from their homes was a quiet young couple, Joseph and Mary, from the Galilean village of Nazareth. They had to make the long and often dangerous journey from their homeland to the place where they could officially register their names for the census. Coming from Nazareth, Jews will tell you, is a handicap in itself, but a journey from Nazareth

to Bethlehem in the depth of winter must
have been a severe ordeal for this couple, for
Mary was pregnant, and the birth of her
child was not far away. In gentle stages –
Joseph walking, Mary riding a donkey –
they covered the ninety-odd miles, and on
24 December, tired and hungry, they
reached their native home, the town of Bethlehem.

It was late when they arrived; it was wet
and cold, and the only hotel in Bethlehem
was already – literally – packed to the
rafters. Aaron Bar Jona is the owner and
manager of the Bethlehem Hotel.

AARON: Look! I'm getting fed up with all these in-
sinuations and suggestions that I turned the
Messiah away from my door. You've got to
look at the realities of the situation. This is
the only hotel in Bethlehem. If I get half a
dozen paying customers it's a good day, but
on this particular night I had forty people
crammed into this house. Most of them just
slept wherever they could get a place to lie
down. Do you have any idea how many
people belong to the tribe of David? And
they all had to come here to register. For two
weeks we were booked solid. I knew when
I saw this young couple from Nazareth that
this was a special case. I could see the condition she was in, but what was I supposed
to do? Put her in a room with fifteen other
people, or maybe ask the other fifteen people to vacate their room because we had visitors from Nazareth? I did the only thing I
could think of. I told them both to go down
to the stables, where at least they would

have heat and privacy. It's not such a bad place, you know. It's only city folk that talk about the animals and the smell and 'surely it cannot be very hygienic'. If you were ever out on the mountains on a cold night, you'd be happy to get into a stable. Ask any farmer who's had to sit up all night with a sick animal.

Anyway, when my wife went down early next morning – to see how they were getting on – there was the baby, sleeping peacefully in the manger, and the mother sitting by its side, just staring at it – sort of fascinated, like you sometimes see mothers with a new baby. The father was over at the door chatting to a couple of shepherds who had apparently arrived during the night. They had some strange story about being warned by angels about the birth of a saviour, but you know what shepherds are like. They can tell some right fairy tales.

JACOB: I'm Jacob Bar Jona. I'm shepherd to Joseph of Bethlehem along with Nathaniel and Reuben. We look after about three hundred sheep, and during the lambing season, we stay out on the hills all night – protection, you know, against wolves and foxes – and then there's always a few light-fingered customers around here who wouldn't think twice about lifting a lamb or two.

Anyway, it must have been about three o' clock in the morning, we were having a bite to eat, when suddenly the whole sky lit up, bright as day, and this voice came out of nowhere saying, 'Don't be afraid. I've brought good news for you. The saviour that you've all been waiting for has been born in David's city' – that's Bethlehem – 'and this is how you will recognise him. He's a baby, wrapped in a blanket and lying in a manger'. And then suddenly the air was filled with voices, all singing together, 'Glory to God in the highest'. Now, don't tell me that I fell asleep before the fire and dreamt it all. I've been out on those hills long enough to know real voices when I hear them – and, anyway, the others heard them as well. I can tell you we were frightened out of our wits, but then it all stopped, as suddenly as it had started, and we found ourselves standing alone on the mountain with our mouths open, staring at each other, wondering what was going on.

It took a while for it all to sink in, but none of us needed much persuasion to leave the mountain and go down to the town to find out what was happening. When we got to Bethlehem we asked some people was there a child born anywhere tonight, and they directed us to the stable, and sure enough, there was the baby, lying in the manger, wrapped in a blanket, exactly like the voice had said.

PHILIP: So far there has been nothing in this affair that cannot be explained by natural cause; and our investigations brought to light another fact which indicates a purely natural explanation for everything that has happened.

Mary has a cousin called Elizabeth, who is married to Zechariah, one of the priestly tribe of Abijah, and fifteen months ago, he was chosen by lottery for the supreme honour of offering incense in the Holy of Holies – the heart of the Jewish Temple. This was a once-in-a-lifetime privilege and the excitement probably took its toll on Zechariah – he was, after all, over seventy years of age – but something happened while he was in the Holy of Holies. Believers say it was a divine vision, others say that he had a stroke, but, at any rate, when he finally reappeared, he was unable to speak. He was hustled off home and some time later an equally unexpected event occurred. His fifty-year-old wife, Elizabeth, conceived a child. To believers, this was the fulfilment of Zechariah's vision, to others it was merely a coincidence. However, it was six months before Mary heard about this pregnancy, and by this time she herself was pregnant, so she immediately rushed off to the hill country of Judah to congratulate her cousin. We spoke to Elizabeth about that eventful meeting.

ELIZABETH: I was so overjoyed about this child of mine. It was an impossible dream come true, and I firmly believed that nothing in this life could ever affect me more than having this child. But when Mary appeared, it was as if the child gave a great leap of joy, and I felt as if I had suddenly encountered something even more tremendous than my own child. It was as if Mary's child were even more wonderful than my own, and without any thinking or planning on my part, the words seemed to come flowing out of me: 'Blessed are you and blessed is your child. Who am I that the mother of the Messiah should come to visit me?'

PHILIP: One can imagine the effect of these words on an impressionable young girl in the early stages of pregnancy. And if these were the only facts available, we would be justified in dismissing the whole affair as the product of overactive imaginations and wishful thinking. But about two weeks after the birth of Mary's child, events took a strange turn. Into Bethlehem rode a strange procession of powerful and wealthy foreigners. Nothing quite like it had ever been seen in Bethlehem before. There were bodyguards and servants and camels piled high with costly provisions and they all converged on the stable beneath the Bethlehem hotel. The locals were either too afraid or too over-awed to speak to them and it was only by retracing these foreigners' footsteps back to Jerusalem and making enquiries there that we were able to discover the identity of one of their leaders – Melchior of Arabia. He had by now returned to his homeland, so we travelled to Arabia and requested an interview. He was not at all anxious to speak to us, but after much negotiation he agreed to tell us his story.

MELCHIOR: The holy books of the Jewish people are quite familiar to us. We know that they fore-tell a leader, a Messiah, who will come to set them free, and we know that his coming will be foretold by strange disturbances in the stars and planets. Unlike you, we have a firm conviction that the celestial bodies have a very definite effect on the outcome of human events, and the precise study of these bodies has long been part of our national culture. It was in the weeks prior to our visit to Judea that we first noticed some strange aberrations from the normal path of stars and planets, and eventually among them a new star appeared, brighter than all the rest and following a set path every night, moving west from our own country and stopping at a precise point each night – according to our calculations precisely over Judea. I sent messengers to some of my neighbouring rulers who also make a study of the stars and found that they too had made the same observations – and had also reached the same conclusion. These were the signs that indicated the birth of the Jewish Messiah. We are not an ungodly people. We see the hand of God in everything we do, and it seemed only right and proper that if God had revealed to us the secrets of his plans we should immediately pay our respects to the messenger of God.

We followed the star every night, and sure enough it brought us to Judea, and there we had to halt because we had no information about where to find the Messiah. It seemed reasonable to visit King Herod, to pay our respects as visitors to his country and to enquire about the birthplace of the Messiah. We naturally assumed that the learned men of Judea had also noticed the disturbance in the elements and that they too had regarded them as a sign of the coming Messiah. We were surprised to find that neither Herod nor his counsellors had any idea of what we were talking about, but he soon called his priests and scribes together and instructed them to search the holy books and find exactly where the Messiah was to be born. They all agreed finally that he would be born in Bethlehem, the city of King David, and we found nothing unusual in King Herod's request that we should return as soon as we had found the Messiah and let him know so that he too could go and pay his respects.

We set off for Bethlehem, and once again the star went ahead of us and finally stopped over the town. There had already been some talk among the locals about the birth of the Messiah, so they were easily able to point out to us the stable in which he was born. You must understand that this was an act of faith on our part. We did not depend on any human calculations or reasons. We followed the star and it led us to a stable, but we were not disturbed or surprised. We went in and, according to our traditions, offered gifts and good wishes to this tiny child. The parents received us graciously and thanked us for our kindness; and when we had rested from our journey we intended to return to our homeland. However, the night before we left, all three of us had the same dream pointing us away from Jerusalem and guiding us home by another route. It was only when we had reached home that we learned the wisdom of our choice; but that was the last time we saw the Messiah.

PHILIP: The choice of route by Melchior and his colleagues was indeed a wise one – at least for their own peace of mind – as the next few days were to prove. At dawn on the third day after their departure, the town of Bethlehem awoke to find itself completely surrounded by a battalion of the Royal Guard. One of the townsmen describes what happened.

TOWNSMAN: A solid line of soldiers, all armed with swords, spears and shields encircled the town, but at first they did nothing. The soldiers merely stood at the ready, legs apart, shields raised, the rising sun glinting off their helmets. At first the people were merely puzzled – some talked about army manoeuvres – but when every second soldier left the ranks and began to converge on the town, they got nervous and began running here and there, calling out to the mayor and the councilmen, 'What's happening? What's wrong?' But the mayor and his colleagues were as mystified as the rest of us, and they merely watched anxiously as the line of soldiers arrived at the first house in their path. A corporal and two privates broke ranks and entered the house, and shortly afterwards came out carrying a small baby, followed by a woman screaming hysterically. While the private soldiers restrained her, the corporal quietly, without any show of emotion, set the child down on the ground, drew his sword and sliced its head off. The soldiers then released the woman, and the line moved off again. No accusations were made, no explanations were given. The soldiers merely entered each house in turn, seized all the baby boys and executed them. Frantic mothers were screaming and throwing themselves upon their children, but the soldiers merely dragged them away and went on with their work until every male child in the entire town was dead.

PHILIP: It was this unprecedented massacre of innocent children that transformed a comparatively local incident into an international outrage and attracted the attention of reporters from all over the empire. Needless to say the civil authorities were playing down the incident as much as possible, and the army was obviously warned to say nothing. Colonel Marcus Drusus, the commanding office of the Royal Guard, refused to be drawn into any comment.

MARCUS DRUSUS: I'm a soldier and a soldier's duty is to obey his lawful civil authority. It is not my duty – nor my inclination – to question orders or to ask for reasons or explanations. As far as I was concerned, this was just another military operation, and my job was to see that it was carried out as promptly and efficiently as possible. I have no further comment to make on the matter.

PHILIP: Colonel Drusus may be able to let the matter rest there, but the weight of public opinion – and especially media pressure from all over the empire – has compelled the civil authorities to take things a little further. Various palace spokesmen tried their hands at justifying the massacre but they were told in no uncertain terms – by the assembled press – that their story did not measure up. So great in fact was the pressure for an explanation that finally, this morning, we were invited to the imperial palace to be addressed at a press conference by King Herod himself.

HEROD: Good morning, gentlemen. At the outset I must say that I am not a little surprised to find that men of your intelligence and experience should find it so hard to reconcile some of the harsher realities of life with the demands of good government. This great country of ours, which has endured so much down the ages, has always had to face up to the dangers that surround it – and that sometimes lie within it. We have many enemies – some on our doorstep – who would like nothing better than the chance to humiliate God's chosen people, and it has been the urgent priority of this government to make sure that our existence as an independent nation and our freedom to practise the faith that we hold so dear should always be protected. That we should accept, and to some extent depend on the patronage of Rome in no way undermines that freedom, for if it should happen that Rome should see fit to withdraw its forces and leave us to the tender mercy of our enemies, I have no doubt that we should quickly cease to exist as a nation and that our fate would be extinction or, at the very least, slavery.

For this reason I have always considered it an essential priority to preserve the stability of this country and to give no one – in Rome or elsewhere – an excuse for interfering in the internal affairs of our nation. I have allowed nothing to take priority over this need – and it has not always been easy, as you well know. I have had to contend not merely with enemies from without but from within – and even from within my own family – and I have allowed nothing, neither ties of blood nor affection, to come between me and the solemn duty I have towards my country. My own sons Alexander and Aristobulus were not spared when they so far forgot their duty as to plot against their own fatherland. I have not spared even my own wife Marianne, nor her grandfather, Joseph, when the security of my country demanded it. I have made supreme sacrifices for my country. I have spared no one who has dared to undermine its stability, and even today, despite my failing health, I still struggle to preserve that stability – and what is my reward? Treachery – betrayal and treachery from those whom I would most reasonably expect to be my friends and my support in my hour of need. Why then should I spare these infants of Bethlehem? Which is more important: the life of this nation or the life of a few infants?

Every pretender to the throne of the Messiah is a threat to the existence of this nation of ours. We must strike them down. We must protect the independent existence of our country or the heroic sacrifices of our forefathers will have been in vain. We must wipe out the traitors and the frauds before they get a chance to betray us. We must spare no one – neither sons nor daughters, infants or ancients, friends or foes –

who would plot against the lawful government of this country. Traitors must be stamped out, they must be destroyed, they must be wiped off the face of the earth ...

PHILIP:

The press conference was terminated at this point, so none of the journalists present was given the chance to point out that, according to the people of Bethlehem, the only infant who was connected in any way with a claim to be the Messiah had left Bethlehem with his father and mother three days before the massacre, and had last been seen heading south in the direction of Egypt. Neither the children who were killed, nor their families, nor anyone remotely connected with them has ever been associated with a claim to be the Messiah – only the child called Jesus, the son of Mary and Joseph of Nazareth, and he is nowhere to be found. The feeling in official circles is that it is all over now – another false claimant to the leadership of Judea has been exposed, or at least frightened off, and peace and tranquillity can return once again to the land. But there are still some believers. Simeon of Emmaus is an old man. He spends a great deal of his time in the Temple praying to God for himself and for his people, but he is a down-to-earth, sensible man according to his neighbours. He has no doubts.

SIMEON:

I have seen the Messiah. He was carried into the temple in his mother's arms only days ago. He was bought back from the Lord, like every first-born, with an offering of doves – for his parents are poor people, unimportant in the eyes of the world – but the Messiah's Kingdom is not of this world. He will not save Judea alone, but he will stretch out his hands to all the peoples of the world and they shall be one people, God's people, united in love for one another and in their worship of the one God.

PHILIP:

This already is a new and dangerous doctrine. No Jew will easily give up his belief that he belongs to God's chosen people and that he stands apart from and above all other peoples. Teachings about universal love and fraternity cannot expect a very warm welcome from him – at least if he is prosperous – but it is an attractive doctrine to the millions of poor and unlettered people who have nothing to lose but their servitude. Until now, the Jewish God has been the patron of the wealthy and powerful. If you prospered it was because God had blessed you. If you suffered it was because God had reason to punish you. Now comes the suggestion that maybe there are other explanations; maybe you prospered because you were more aggressive or more ruthless than anyone else, and God had little to do with it.

If a doctrine like that were to take root and find favour with the people, it could have devastating effects, and this doctrine stems from that most unlikely Messiah of all, the baby who was born in Bethlehem. One can only ask, if this infant can throw the Jewish authorities into such turmoil while he is still in the cradle, what kind of turmoil will he not create when he grows to be a man?

Obituaries

JP McClarey

By any reasonable standards, Christmas should be a frightening time. We are, after all, receiving into our midst the Son of God, and we all know how much effort we put into preparing for important visitors. Whether it is prospective in-laws, or bosses from work, or indeed any kind of influential or successful person who seems to have risen above us, whether in Church or state or school, we tend to tighten up to some degree when we have to meet them.

But here we are, waiting for the Son of God to come among us, and there is no sign of nerves or tension or fear. We look forward to his coming with joy because he presents no threat. He will not harm us or undermine us or frighten us in any way because he is just a little baby in a cradle. He wanted to be sure that we were not frightened, so he made himself helpless. He made himself incapable of doing harm to anyone. And this is the same Son of God who will come again to meet us at the end of time, only this time he will come to judge us, to determine what will become of us for eternity. Is it likely that someone who has made such sacrifices for our sake, who has left behind the splendour and the power of his real existence lest it frighten us in any way, will not put up a strong fight to save us from eternal death? If we have welcomed Christ at his first coming throughout our lives, is it likely that he will not welcome us at his second coming? Will not those who have reached out to Christ throughout their lives be welcomed by him at the hour of their death?

JP McClarey, throughout his life, has reached out to Christ instinctively and faithfully because it was a way of life, a culture of faith into which he was born and raised, and which he regarded as something to be preserved and promoted. His dedication to prayer and to the practice of his faith was not some superimposed addition or decoration to life, but an integral and most natural component of life itself. To live without faith – and the practice of his faith – would be as unthinkable, and indeed impossible, as living without food to eat or air to breathe. JP's life was immersed in his religion in much the same way as it was immersed in the sights and smells and memories of his birthplace, Glenburn House. He was not only born there, he was married from there, and there he reared his family, and it was a measure of the inner peace and serenity his wife and family brought him that he never felt the urge to live anywhere else, or even to spend too much time away from the familiar and reassuring sights and sounds of home. The best part of holidays – if indeed they had to be tolerated – was, in his estimation, getting back home again. Instead of travel his delight was to experiment with his beloved apple trees and to attend to all the variations of stock and crops that were at the heart of his farming, and when all was done to stack away neatly and tidily in shed or cupboard all the tools of his trade in preparation for a new day's work tomorrow.

In his later years he had the look and the manner of an ideal grandfather; a slightly heavy build, a slow deliberate step, a good head of hair and a very droll sense of humour. One couldn't help thinking that if the advertising experts had got their hands on him they could have sold Hovis bread by the lorryload. His pastime was football – or maybe it would be more accurate to say that his obsession was football; as a player in his young days and as a supporter and spectator in his later years. He followed the fortunes of Tottenham Hotspur through good times and bad and would hear no evil spoken of them. Manchester United, on the other hand, he regarded – and rightly so, in my unbiased opinion – as a collection of prima donnas, and that included the manager.

He enjoyed spectacular health for eighty years, and endured patiently the pains and privations of his final illness. Even then he was a presence, whether in his sickbed or in his home or in his parish. He did not need to say or do anything. He was simply there, and you were aware of him. He calmly and courageously accepted God's will when the end came in sight, and declared himself ready to go whenever it might suit the Almighty to call him.

He will be greatly missed by Angela and Damien and Frances, but the memories they share of a good and loving man will sustain them in the days that lie ahead. We all mourn his passing, for he was truly a pillar of this parish, and we pray that God will forgive any failings and take due account of all his goodness, and bring him at the end to the joy of God's Kingdom in Heaven.

Isabel McLaughlin

The human race never ceases to search for the truth. That, of course, does not mean that every member of the human race is consistently and consciously searching for the truth, but it does mean that there will always be men and women who continually probe and investigate the reality behind every other reality, in an attempt to come to some deeper and clearer understanding of it.

Every generation has sought the truth, and in every generation someone has claimed to have found it – but with the passage of time they begin to suspect that maybe their truth is not as reliable as they once thought it was. We see it most clearly in matters of health. In one decade we are told that a daily aspirin tablet will keep our arteries open. A decade later we are told that it is now deemed a questionable remedy. The glass of red wine that was supposed to be good for our heart is now dismissed as a pious excuse for indulging. What used to be called a healthy tan is now classed as reckless exposure. Every generation does what every other generation has done before it – they allow intellectual pride to mistake a tiny fragment of truth for the whole structure. And because they are so convinced by the fragment of truth they have discovered they refuse to believe that you too may have discovered your own fragment of truth. Only honest and open-minded individuals are willing to accept that if I listen and absorb your fragment of truth along with my own I am now twice as wise as I was beforehand.

You might well ask at this point, 'Where is this long-winded introduction leading us?', and the simplest answer is that it helps to explain the open-mindedness and the balance and the wisdom of Isabel McLaughlin. She absorbed the truths and the culture of the Church of Ireland into which she was born and reared and carried them into the Catholic faith and culture in which she spent her married life, and she was an outstanding credit to both of them.

We are all formed and fashioned by the culture in which we are reared, and that culture is a combined product of our home life and our spiritual life. If you have been taught consideration and restraint in your youth you will retain it into your more mature years. If you have been taught to put your trust in God and to worship him as his Son Jesus Christ has taught us, then you will carry that respect for your faith and for your God into whatever regions life may take you. Isabel carried her faith and her culture into every corner of life.

It is said that the hallmark of a good magician is the ability to make the most difficult tricks look easy, and Isabel McLaughlin made rearing nine children look easy. She always gave the impression that she had matters in hand, that she knew what she was doing and that there was no need – nor indeed any justification – for any fuss or worry. And if any confirmation of this were needed it was to be found in the happy atmosphere that pervaded her home at all times. She did not worry that her kitchen might not have an island or that there was no granite worktop or solid oak cupboards. Instead, she worried that you had a cup of tea in your hand and that you felt comfortable.

For her children the future must seem bleak, but all is not darkness. There are a few rays of hope and comfort to be found in the memory of the loving mother she has been to them, and all the good things that she has done for them. They will look back on the wonderful days of their youth and not merely relive them in memory but, hopefully, they will try to recreate those days in their own lives and pass them on to their children and to their grandchildren. Some foolish expert has suggested that parental management of the home and the maintenance of respect among children is a relic of a bygone age, when in fact children have always instinctively seen reasonable discipline as a sign that they are loved and cared for.

Isabel handled life quietly and methodically, and she handled sickness and death in the same way. There were no complaints, no demands, no outbursts. Just a peaceful acceptance of what God has determined. 'The Lord has given. The Lord has taken away. Blessed be the name of the Lord'.

She lived her entire life within a three-mile radius of Drumrammer, yet she had more wisdom and more awareness of the world than some who have circled the globe. She will be sadly missed by all her children, but then she will be sadly missed by all of us.

I looked for some word or phrase that might summarise her personality – if such is possible – and it was only when I heard someone else describe her that I knew that I had found the right words. You have often heard the expression 'Christian gentleman'. Well, Isabel was the perfect example of the 'Christian lady'.

May the Lord acknowledge all her goodness and virtue. May he speedily forgive any faults. May he accept her into his Kingdom and grant her eternal happiness, and may he comfort and console all those left behind to mourn her.

Gerry Keown

God our Father gives us many reasons to be positive in the face of death, but even with the best of intentions and the most exemplary acceptance of God's will, we cannot describe a burial as anything other than a sad and tragic occasion. Death is always devastating, but the battle to defeat or even postpone death can be so wearing for everyone that when death finally strikes it leaves us in a state of utter exhaustion. It is as if we have been wrestling with death in deadly combat and, despite all our efforts, death has won.

Six months ago, when Gerry's illness was diagnosed, he confronted it, as he did other things in life, in a direct and positive way. Illness was illness, but it was not invincible. It could be cured; and if it wasn't curable it was certainly containable, so there was always the prospect not just of months but of years of remission, and in the meantime who knows what might happen? In the hallowed traditions of Irish manhood, he spoke little about the mortal implications of his sickness. That was reserved for another day when hope of healing had faded and new dilemmas had to be faced. It was his way of being courageous in the face of death and it did not for a moment evade the heavy choices that have to be made as life runs down.

His faith was the business-like faith that the writer Graham Greene demanded from his Church – a logical sequence of prayers, Mass and devotions that leads one forward into the heart of one's faith, until eventually there is no alternative but to let go. For his generation, it was not enough to feel good before God, to have pleasant spiritual experiences, it must also make sense. It must follow definite instructions from God, whether to pray or to ask or to seek, and whatever features and aspects of life might seem dark or confused, they will be duly revealed in clarity and light in the Kingdom of God.

Gerry's death is significant for all of us because he is the first of his generation to be called away – at least from where we in the Collins family stand. Four of my sisters married within the space of two years, so it was a common sight to see four prospective sons-in-law assembled at the one time in the old house in Coneywarren. They did not have an easy time of it – the rules may have been unwritten but they applied as though carved in granite. My mother – Granny Collins, as she later came to be known – had a completely impartial attitude to all her future sons-in-law. She made no distinction of person or position between the four of them. She regarded them all as equally useless.

This was not through any fault of personality or performance on their part. It was simply that they were outsiders. They came from a different town and that was obviously a drawback. They grew up in a different family environment and that was obviously a handicap. If they smoked they were spendthrifts. If they drank they were – potentially at least – alcoholic. If they did neither they were devious; they were probably concealing even greater vices under the appearance of virtue. It was against this stark background that Gerry had to prove himself, but it presented little difficulty. His seriousness of purpose and his meticulousness in planning were soon apparent, and by the time the grandchildren arrived he was not merely accepted but frequently held up as an example of what a son-in-law should be.

Gerry's relationship with my father, on the other hand, was always a more relaxed affair, which is surprising, because Gerry's work involved numerous aspects of health and social service ministry, not least the dreaded job of dole man. My father, on the other hand, regarded the right to work and draw the dole as every true Irishman's birthright, since one had a civic duty to lever as much unearned money from the government as possible.

These roles were accidentally reversed on one occasion when my father visited Teresa and Gerry in Enniskillen. He wanted to visit a farming friend of his some miles away, so he took a loan of Gerry's car. As he approached the farm he saw large numbers of men and boys picking potatoes in the field beside the house. As he turned into the lane the men dropped their baskets and boxes and bolted for the far hedge, which they hurdled like hardened steeple-chasers, and disappeared from view. As my father reached the house a very relieved looking farmer fervently invoked the holy name and told him that when they saw the car they thought it was that expeditious dole man Gerry Keown, except that his language was a great deal more earthy and colourful.

Gerry came up in the culture of his generation where you kept your ear to the ground and your shoulder to the wheel, where you cared for your own, where you saved for the rainy day. You might indulge your children but not yourself. You had to be sensible and responsible. It was not a luxurious life but it was an involved and committed life. He was a font of wisdom and guidance to his family and supported them in all their endeavours. He was a strong traditional member and supporter of his faith and his Church, and through it and through his family he created many deep and precious relationships with those he has left behind. In the Kingdom of God he can look forward to the fulfilment and the perfection of these relationships, for eternal life holds no joy for us unless we can share it with the people who have been an important part of our lives here on earth. The great joy is that the earthly imperfections in these relationships will have been rectified, the flaws will have been repaired, the mistakes will have been corrected. All that remains is the perfect but personal joy of being reunited once more with someone whom we have loved in this life, and that is why we try to live according to God's law so that we will eventually be joined together forever in that Kingdom where there is no death but only lasting peace.

Sally Loughrey

In this life on earth most of us try to live according to the commandments of God. We don't always succeed, for apart from anything else, we tend to concentrate on certain commandments to the neglect of others, but we do try to respond to them all, so that even when we fall by the wayside we still consider ourselves to be Christians – not outstanding Christians, you understand, but sincere and committed Christians.

And then there are the people who do not concentrate on the commandments. Instead, they try to live by the Beatitudes, and that is a completely different programme altogether. The commandments are reasonable and understandable directives. We can see the sense of loving God and our neighbour and not stealing or committing adultery and so on. But there is no sense to the Beatitudes. 'Blessed are the poor in spirit, blessed are the meek, blessed are those who mourn, blessed are those who are persecuted'. 'What is blessed about all these?' The answer is short and simple. 'Your reward will be great in Heaven'. Those who live by the Beatitudes have a head start on the rest of us when it comes to knocking on the door of Heaven.

Sally Loughrey lived her life by the Beatitudes. From an early age she learned the price that one had to pay not merely to survive but to succeed in a world of poverty and hardship. Rights and privileges were unheard of. Working conditions were the maximum labour for the minimum wage. She was hired out to a strange family in a strange town, at the age of fourteen, far from her home in Sistrakeel, but she determined early on that this was not how she was going to spend her life. She returned home and later began housekeeping work with a local family and shortly afterwards met her future husband, around whom the rest of her life revolved. I always suspected that she was the power behind the throne, as it were, but only recently did I discover just how energetic and enterprising she was. Where someone else might have claimed that rearing a family in such harsh economic times was sufficient hardship to impose on anyone, Sally asked herself 'How do we improve these economic conditions?' and set up a little shop which she maintained and ran for many years to come.

Combined with this business sense was an overarching charity that took everyone into account. In this world there are givers and takers, and beyond any shadow of a doubt Sally Loughrey was a giver. Until I came to Limavady, I hadn't known her, though I had met some of her children briefly, but it was when I came here that I began to see the natural generosity by which she lived, and the attention that she devoted not merely to her family but to everyone around her. Every Saturday evening she and Mary would land up at the parochial house with a home-cooked wheaten scone – and sometimes even more exotic items. It was such a thoughtful gesture, I felt. In fact I regarded it as a memorable gesture, for a gift that we have created with our own hands is so much more meaningful than what we have just bought over the counter. And it had nothing to do with food, really. I don't think Sally thought that there was any danger of me passing away from hunger during my time in Limavady, though it was a welcome addition to the larder. It was a gesture of friendship, an indication that she had not forgotten me, and in a life that is becoming increasingly solitary and isolated it is so important that you feel you have not been forgotten, that you are not just another cog in the parochial wheel, but that somehow you deserve to be remembered.

As I said, giving came naturally to her, and she gave generously to her children and to her extended family, but when it came to giving to her husband Jim all the stops were pulled out, all the limitations were overlooked, for the only really important thing in her life was his happiness. Jim was deserving of such care; for all his life he had dedicated himself to the parish of Limavady, looking out for those among his fellow parishioners who were going through hard times, but also caring for needy members of other denominations without distinction. It was this dedication which led to his nomination for the Benemerenti Medal, and as I look back on my days in Limavady I can say that nothing gives me quite the same satisfaction as the bestowal of such a high honour on Jim Loughrey.

As I said, nothing came before Jim's welfare in Sally Loughrey's estimation. She stated quite bluntly that her only ambition was to survive long enough to care for him until his last day. This she achieved, though I wonder did she believe that God would take her so literally when Jim died at the table beside her.

There is so much more to her life, but let me finish by saying that she was a good wife and mother, she was a good neighbour, she was a good parishioner, she was a good Christian, and by now I am quite sure that she is baking scones and making tea in the anterooms of Heaven, in welcome for all the friends that knew her in this life.

Johnny Kearney

If we take the phrase 'my yoke is easy and my burden light', our instinctive reaction is to reject it, for experience has taught us that in most instances, the yoke will be awkward and the burden heavy. There are, however, exceptions, and in the past few days, by a strange coincidence, I have come across two situations where this lesson was taught with very convincing clarity.

In the first instance, Johnny Kearney, whom we bury here this morning, cared for his wife who suffered from MS for many years, and dedicated himself to making life as comfortable for her as he could in the circumstances. It was not that he found the burden heavy – in fact this became the centre around which his life revolved, and the care of his wife became the fulfilment of all his desires and ambitions. In very truth the yoke became easy and the burden light.

By a very strange coincidence, forty miles away in another parish at this very moment, my cousin is burying his wife of forty-two years, thirty-eight of which he spent caring for her because of the ravages of MS. His entire life was dedicated to her care. Someone foolishly suggested that he would find some rest after his labours now that she was dead. His reaction was very emphatic indeed. The very idea that – somehow – he could be happy in any situation that did not involve her seemed completely foreign to him. He had given his life to caring for her, and in that caring he found great fulfilment and a strange kind of – not enjoyment – but satisfaction that no other form of activity could have supplied. His commitment to her was so complete that anything involving her evoked an immediate and wholehearted reaction. It was his joy to serve her, and in that way he found his yoke was easy and his burden light.

That same experience will be part of the experience of the family of Johnny Kearney, who have cared for and looked after him in such dedicated fashion over recent years. The idea that the giving of oneself to another will be a burden from which we hope to be released never works out that way. It is in fact a commitment to which we feel dedicated, and when we are no longer able to fulfil it, it leaves an enormous emptiness and gap in our lives.

For the daughters of Johnny Kearney in the days to come there will be this strange emptiness, this strange awareness that there is part of their lives missing, and yet they will not be able to quantify it, nor even to personify it, but they will definitely experience it. For Johnny Kearney was not just another dedicated and loving father. His life revolved around his wife and his children, and they experienced the joy of his involvement and appreciated the warmth and the strength of his personality, and the way in which he passed on to them everything he experienced from his work in the wider world.

While some might see the vocation of a bar manager as somewhat limited, those who have experience of the world will quickly point out that there is no more effective school for life than a few years spent behind the counter of a bar serving drinks. I had the good fortune to have a curate for ten years whose parents owned a bar, and all during holiday time in his youth, like it or not, he was compelled to serve behind the counter, and in doing so he acquired an education that the rest of us could only envy. He acquired an ability to communicate with people and to understand their weaknesses and strengths and how to persuade them to do the right thing rather than simply put pressure on them to follow his demands. He learned more about human nature behind the counter of his father's bar than the rest of us did from seven years of studying the esoteric ramifications of theology and philosophy.

It has been my misfortune to have known Johnny only in more recent years, but as one listens to those who were friendly with him in his younger days, it is quite clear that he was an exceptional man. He would seem to have acquired the ability not just to communicate with people, but to interact with them and to be an intermediary in so many different aspects of life. One tends to think of a barman as someone whose unhappy responsibility it is to keep an eye on the troublemakers and to evict those patrons who are creating more than their fair share of disruption and causing a degree of unhappiness among the regular customers. Johnny seems to have had the great gift of persuading even those who were well over the limit that they should be taking themselves home under their own steam rather than being sent on their way by any exercise of force or violence. Even those who now acknowledge that their consumption of alcohol was beyond any reasonable limits and their behaviour somewhat erratic by any standards admit that Johnny was always sensitive and understanding, and always tried to solve the problem in a gentle way rather than by any use of force or threats.

In his last illness he was the essence of patience and acceptance. He never complained or burdened those around him with demands for better treatment. If he could put a cheerful face upon it he did, and he accepted the fact that age was encroaching upon him with equanimity. Death was merely another step on the journey.

He will be greatly missed by his family, his friends and his parish. We commend his kindly soul to God and pray that he will be granted eternal rest.

Jane McNickle

The greatest human loss through death is the death of a spouse –
the death of a husband or wife – and after that comes the death of
a mother. Husbands and wives – in the ideal situation – live their
lives so close to one another. They have shared so many profound
experiences together, they have endured so much pain and trauma
together, they have laughed and rejoiced in the successes they have
achieved together, and they have cried and lamented at the failures
and the disappointments they have suffered together, and in the
process they have come to know one another so intimately and so
profoundly that when death comes it is as though one had not just
lost a friend but a part of one's self.

The closest to that experience, in terms of trauma and confusion,
is the death of a mother. In our naivety we try to anticipate such a
loss and even convince ourselves that we have analysed and
explained the process to ourselves. We have lived our own lives
for so many years, we tell ourselves; we have our own house, we
have a job, we have a family and we barely have time to think of
others, even when they are comparatively young and healthy, but
when their years have lengthened and their limbs have grown frail
and unsteady, we tell ourselves that their lives have ceased to
impinge upon ours, that we have coped without them for this or
that number of years and so their death will not make any great
difference to our own life programme. We will acknowledge the
fact of their death, and then pass on. Nothing could be more false.
The person whom we have lost is not defined by a few final years
of infirmity, but by every moment of life from birth to death.

Jane McNickle's family was shaped and moulded by the entire ninety-two years of her life. They began in childhood where she was a strong loving presence, completely dedicated to her home and her children. They were given love and guidance and security, and probably thought to themselves, 'This is how every family is cared for'. Then they moved to the teenage years and the inevitable conflict of wills that accompanies them. They probably discovered that it would take a lifetime of careful scheming to outwit her. She didn't raise her voice, she didn't threaten you with dire retribution. She merely looked into your eyes and read your personality from A to Z with an effortless grace that left you convinced that she knew all your sins even when she didn't, which was rarely.

Then, into the adult years, and here she would have been a fountain of wisdom and discretion. As a wife and mother she would have dealt with most problems in her time, and as communications between mother and children grew more natural and relaxed she would have passed on the distilled wisdom of her own experience and guided them into the best course of action. There were some who said that she had assured her eternal salvation by marrying a cattle dealer, for anyone who cared for a cattle dealer for all those years had undoubtedly served their time and done penance for their sins.

As her family grew to middle age she grew into old age, and became, not a power in their lives any more but a presence. She was the centre of family life, the focus of every gathering and the heart of every celebration. She sat in her chair by the window and her children and her grandchildren and the rest of the world passed in respectful procession before her. I cannot say if she was ever angry but she always greeted me with a smile even on those days when she didn't know who I was. Her faith was rock solid. I have no doubt that she lived it with attentive devotion, because in her final years, while she may have been confused or incoherent about worldly matters, when you said, 'In the name of the Father' or 'The Body of Christ', she immediately came alive and joined in the prayers with fervour.

Great credit must go to her family and to the carers who looked after her in her final years. I know that Bridgeen Deehan will be greatly distressed to hear of her death for her one wish before leaving for Australia was that Jane would not die until she got back. However, God has his own timetable, and we must learn to adapt.

Her passing will leave a strange and massive emptiness in the hearts of her family and friends, and they will marvel at how deeply her death has affected them. And there is no quick cure. The healing process must be a natural one, which is why the Scriptures speak to us about patience and trust. 'The Lord is good to those who trust him, to the soul that searches for him. It is good to wait in silence for the Lord to save'.

Brigid McLaughlin

We used to have a picture of saints as boring stereotypes from the middle ages who were sinless from the first day of their birth. Their biographers tried to tell us that they spent long hours in contemplative prayer from their very childhood and the thought of committing a sin was something that never crossed their minds. And if by some freakish misfortune they were actually guilty of some minor peccadillo they spent long hours in penitential exercises, calling on God to forgive them for their appalling failures and promising never to offend again. They were such obnoxious little brats that they gave saints a bad name and even brought childhood into disrepute.

Nowadays, thank God, we take a more down-to-earth view of our faith and begin by acknowledging that no one is perfect, that even the most dedicated followers of Christ will occasionally break loose and follow their selfish instincts rather than the word of God. The saints of today will try to live out the ideals handed down to them by their faith and their family. They will live firmly in the world but will refuse to be overpowered by the ways of the world.

It was this kind of sanctity that Brigid McLaughlin displayed during her long life. She left home at an early age and went to England, for that was where the work was to be found, even though war was raging around her, and life and limb were in danger from the Blitz. Taking shelter from the bombs in a wardrobe may, however, have been pushing divine providence a bit far.

She came home and married and reared a large family and, as with everything else, she dedicated herself totally and completely to their welfare. The death of Rita must have been a very severe blow to her, and followed by the death of Terry a relatively short time later it brought home to her the frailty of our lives here on earth and their brevity, no matter how long we live.

She had a cast-iron faith in God. It was not so much that she believed in God. It was more that she was on first name terms with God and she didn't hesitate to question his judgement. When her final illness began to take hold she had her good days and her bad days, and on her bad days she would have been quite content to leave this world at any moment, but the Lord kept calling her back for another while, and she was not wildly impressed by his judgement. If she was ready to go there seemed little point in sitting around waiting for this unpredictable day.

She was blessed to be surrounded by family and friends and by loving carers who made her final weeks and months as peaceful and as comfortable as possible. They will all miss her greatly, but their loss is not a private loss, for a parish and a community which has lost someone like her has also suffered a severe bereavement.

Anna Forrester

You are all very welcome to this sad occasion, especially those of you who have come a distance and those of you who are members of other Christian churches.

Let me begin by expressing my deep and sincere sympathy to Gary and to all Anna's brothers and sisters – Maureen, Eugene, Brian, Carmel, Bernie and Peter. The death of Anna, coming so soon after the death of her mother, has made the past eight months a grim and difficult time for all of them. We can only admire the dedication and the compassion with which they handled matters, and we ask God to console and reward them for the sacrifices they have made.

For myself, I can only say that it seems all wrong that Anna should be dead and that I should be attending her funeral, when in fact it would make much more sense if the roles were reversed. That people who are engraved on my mind and in my memory as young people should be dying – and there have been several since I returned here – is hard to absorb and must place a far heavier burden of grief on their friends and families than those who die in old age. But all deaths are traumatic and take their toll on those who are left behind to mourn them.

I first knew Anna many years ago when she – and a few other adventurous souls – used to attend meetings of the Legion of Mary in the old parochial house. I don't think we could claim to be the holiest branch in the organisation. A lot of time was spent making tea and catching up on the news – or, as a less charitable critic put it, 'gossiping and scandalising your neighbours'. Even so, we learned about life and commitment and forgiveness in a way that stayed with us when other lessons were forgotten, and while the rest of us may have allowed our tongues to wag without restraint, the notable thing about Anna was that she didn't talk a great deal – either about herself or anyone else. She was essentially a quiet person.

Inevitably it came to an end, but we always kept in touch – by design at Christmas, and by accident on many other occasions. I was moved to another parish. Anna went to work in Desmonds and moved to Dungiven shortly after Gary was born, and there she remained for more than thirty years in her little house in Priory Road.

She was an excellent worker and moved up the promotional ladder in Desmonds, finally becoming a purchasing officer in Drumahoe, before the factories were finally closed and moved abroad. A huge number of jobs were lost at that time, making it very difficult to find new work, but Anna soon found a position with David Forgie in Limavady, where I would have been a frequent customer and where I often met her, and there she remained until sickness forced her to give up work. But it is an indication of the esteem in which she was held by David Forgie that he kept the position open and assured her that once her health allowed her to return the job was waiting for her.

Her illness may have been obscured by the death of her mother eight months ago and by lesser ailments which had troubled her for some time. I tend to think she kept quiet in case it might have disturbed her mother to know that she was ill. When the seriousness of her illness was finally determined it was too late to take any effective action. But it was at this point that Anna's real strength of character was fully revealed.

Confronted by death she set about preparing for it. The same kind of methodical efficiency that she brought to her work she now brought to putting her affairs in order. Everything from funeral arrangements to souvenir gifts for the family were taken care of, and nothing remained but to await the arrival of death itself. But even here she defied all predictions. It seemed on many occasions that she was about to die, and family and friends waited apprehensively for the message or the phone call that would tell them it was finally over, only to be told that Anna was sitting out in the sun reading the newspaper or having her toenails painted; and for eight weeks she went from crisis to crisis, surviving everything that life could throw at her; but inevitably her energy was declining and she grew more exhausted with each day until she passed away on Friday morning.

I cannot finish without expressing my admiration for her family, and especially Maureen, for the way in which they cared for Anna during her illness, and especially their tireless sensitivity to all Anna's desires. It has been a marathon task but they never wavered in their dedication.

We give thanks to God for the good things in Anna's life. We ask forgiveness for any faults. And we pray that Gary and all the family will be consoled and strengthened by the Spirit of God in the days ahead.

Susan Lynch

In order to prepare this sermon I have had to go back fifty years and examine some of the burdens and the gradual multiplication of expectations that I imposed on Susan Lynch over the years, for, as some of you may know from experience, there is no more inconvenient occurrence than the arrival of a priest on your doorstep without prior warning; and not just a priest making a passing visit but one who gradually makes himself at home in your home, until after repeated visits, and whether he realises it or not, he has made a kind of immobile bollard of himself in the middle of the living room, around which everyone and everything else has to navigate. It doesn't matter that there are six children to be fed, not to mention washed, dressed and supervised, nor does it matter that one of them has fallen and cut his knee and is now leaving a trail of blood around the kitchen floor, or that two others have declared war upon each other and are tearing hanks of hair out of each other's heads. Once the priest arrives the appearance of quiet normality has to be established and maintained until he eventually departs.

His complete lack of domestic experience means that he has no awareness of these critical situations. He does not expect them to occur in the normal household and assumes that the peaceful serenity that he encounters on his arrival is the kind of peaceful atmosphere that will pervade any respectable Christian home. As the years pass and his visits multiply, his expectations move from being served evening tea to getting a bed for the night, so that the disruption and the chaos that he creates now increases and multiplies in geometric progression. At least that is how it was in my day.

All of which would probably submerge the average woman under a tide of conflicting duties, but for Susan Lynch, caring for the multitude was a normal and daily experience. Somehow or other there was always enough to feed the five thousand, or whatever number arrived without warning, and always a bed to accommodate the unannounced visitor – usually myself.

Susan was used to working with large numbers from her childhood. She came from a large family – the sixth successive girl in a family of eleven, and enjoyed a frugal but carefree upbringing where music and entertainment were part of the regular routine. She left school aged fourteen, like everyone else at that time, and went to work in Desmonds shirt factory in Claudy, a place where she learned the fundamentals of dressmaking and also thoroughly enjoyed the life, the work and the company. Even so, the urge to travel which became part of her later life struck early and drew her to a housekeeping job in Solihull for about six months, but she returned home and shortly afterwards made the biggest and wisest decision of her lifetime. Despite having, according to some of her siblings, a tendency to play the field, she eventually singled out and agreed to marry Dan Lynch, and on Boxing Day 1951, she and her sister Kitty married brothers Dan and Packie Lynch. In the best traditions of successful marriage, she and Dan were opposites. Where Susan was constantly exploring the boundaries and looking for ways to expand the horizons, Dan was questioning the need for any change or alteration. If the wallpaper was still sticking to the wall, he found great difficulty understanding the need to remove it and replace it with another type of wallpaper. In fact, on one occasion his opposition to such unnecessary extravagances was so intense that Susan had to strip the walls of a room while he was at work and apply the new wallpaper before he arrived home. Fortunately, Dan never even noticed that the wallpaper had been changed.

She and Dan were very lucky to be allocated a house in Park, which they moved into shortly after their marriage and where they have lived together for the past sixty-three years. Six children followed eventually, and to this day the family recall their childhood in Park, as part of the larger community of children who lived in the cottages, as a time of great diversion and happiness. Discipline was relaxed, but if it had to be imposed Susan had no hesitation about applying it with a sally rod round the back of the legs. Dan was a more lenient disciplinarian. He tended to punish the wrongdoer, and then bribe the victim to stop crying with pennies for sweets.

Susan cultivated a regime of self-sufficiency in order to stretch a single pay packet all through the week by baking her own bread and making a great deal of the clothes for herself and the children, while Dan brought home the potatoes and vegetables that he grew nearby, and provided turf for cooking and heating. Susan even supplemented the weekly income by catering for the farmers and dealers at Park Fair. In fact her domestic economy was so impressive that I once asked her to address a parent meeting in Limavady on the subject of how to feed a family of eight on ten pounds a week.

She took driving lessons at the age of fifty-nine and after five unsuccessful attempts she finally got her licence when she was sixty-four. This opened the way to Derry and other shopping centres and the discovery of charity shops, where, if she did not find the garment she wanted, she could always buy the materials and make up her own outfits at home. The only unsuccessful purchase was a genuine fur coat, which looked perfect, but which her daughters rejected because it did not have a sufficiently swanky label.

In her early years she had little opportunity of travelling or seeing other places, but when the family had grown up and left home she had time on her hands. With their support she was able to visit America and Canada, which she thoroughly enjoyed, and also to make various pilgrimages to Lourdes and Medjugorje. Her final adventure was to share a Mediterranean cruise with some of her family, where, I would imagine, she relished the new experience of having someone else cook and serve the meals.

Her good health lasted into her eighties, but for the last five or six years of her life she was restricted to a wheelchair or even to bed. Most of these years were spent at home, where Dan, with the help of family, nurses and carers, looked after her faithfully until her peaceful death on Sunday. She was a loving wife and mother. She was a faithful member of her Church and of her parish. She was a good neighbour to all around her. We who are gathered here this morning can only join in giving thanks to God for her goodness and ask God to speedily forgive any faults.

Sheila Mullan

Easter Sunday is the central feast of our Christian faith. It is the day on which our fear of eternal death was finally conquered and our belief that we are destined for eternal happiness with God our Father was affirmed. It is therefore a day of rejoicing, a day on which we sing 'Alleluia' in celebration of Christ's victory, and our victory, over death.

And yet we cannot help but ask, 'How can anyone rejoice in the face of the immense tragedy which the Mullan family has suffered today? How can we even talk about coping, much less rejoicing, when a husband has today lost such a good wife and a family has lost such a good mother?'

The rejoicing that we speak of is not the carefree rejoicing of people celebrating some happy event. It is the quiet, unspoken joy that comes from a deep and loving relationship which has perhaps encountered some difficulty. There is pain, but there is assurance that it will survive this and any other obstacle that comes its way. It is because Christ has risen from the dead, it is because we celebrate this feast of Easter, that the Mullan family will be able to leave this church with the assurance that death is not the end, that their close and loving relationship with Sheila will continue, but on a different level, and with an assurance that they will all be reunited in the Kingdom of God.

I have only known Sheila Mullan for a few short years, but it feels like I have lost a lifelong friend. She was such a likeable individual, always pleasant, always smiling, welcoming and hospitable, full of concern for her mother and her family, working each day at a pace that took no account of her own comfort, and committed to her faith and her Church in a way that one can only envy. She was the ideal spiritual person. She was holy, but never stuffy. So often the piety that we see repels rather than attracts us, but Sheila was different. Her piety, like her personality, was always cheerful. If there was a holy hour, or a novena, or some occasion of prayer or devotion, Sheila was sure to be there, quietly praying for all her intentions, most of which were for other people in their various difficulties. She was always conscious of the trials and troubles of those around her, whether family, neighbours or the wider world. She kept them all in her prayers, and in the meantime she worked without pause for the comfort and well-being of those close to her.

It is no surprise that she died with her rosary in her hand. In every difficulty her instinct was to reach out to God in prayer, so we can be quite certain that God heard her final prayer and reached out to welcome her into his Kingdom.

God does not make mistakes. He does not call us from this world at the wrong time. In her comparatively short life Sheila had done so much more and moved so much closer to God than the rest of us that she could afford to leave this world early. We have lost such a good person and such a good parishioner. We pray that God will acknowledge all her goodness, that he will speedily forgive any faults, and that he will accept her into his Kingdom to enjoy there the reward of eternal life. And we pray that God will strengthen and console Micky and his family, and her mother and sister and brothers and all those who have been affected by this sad loss.

Bill Reeves

During the month of November, it is our custom to remember the souls of the dead, and last Friday we gathered to offer Mass for the repose of the souls of those who died in our parish during the past year. As the list of thirty-seven names was read out, we recognised the men and women, the young and the old, the healthy and the infirm, the unexpected and the long-awaited deaths that made up that list, and we wondered, 'How many of them did we expect to find on this list when it began a year ago?'

We have all known situations where the apparently healthy spouse has died while the sick partner, the invalid of the two, lives on. We have also watched the shrinking energy and mobility of the old and prepared ourselves for the onset of death, only to be shocked by the death of some younger and healthier neighbour. We acknowledge all these experiences and we accept them as part of the unpredictability of life, but we never really experience it in our hearts until we lose someone who has been a central pillar of our entire lives.

I knew Bill Reeves long before I came to Limavady. We both had an interest in auctions and we were at an age when we felt justified in squandering a few hours in search of the memorable bargain. Whatever success Bill may have had did not rub off on me. I was the kind of client auctioneers secretly rejoiced to see – a well-meaning innocent out of his depth. Bill was the eternal quiet Englishman, saying little but scanning the goods for a possible investment and responding politely in his strange accent. He survived the auction world much longer than myself, for he made fewer mistakes and kept in mind that eternal truth: 'The auctioneer collects from buyer and seller'.

When I came to Limavady I learned a great deal more about him. Like many another Limavady man he started life in the RAF and met a Limavady girl. And one would assume that he married the Limavady girl and settled down in Limavady and that was that. But not Bill. His Limavady girl went off to work in England so Bill had to follow her there and marry her there and start a family there and only then return to Limavady.

The rest of his life was spent in Limavady. Thirty years in Lilac Avenue and more recently in Bell's Hill. The quiet tenor of Bill's life is best summed up in the only diary he ever kept, and that was for the year 1959 when he and Betty were hoping to start a family. There are only two entries for the whole year. The first reads 'Expecting Janet Patricia'. The second reads 'Janet Patricia born, 6 lb 4 oz'. Bill's delight was in his family, especially the younger children. His grandchildren were a source of great joy to him. He was happy to let the outside world believe that he was outnumbered and overruled by women in his home, but I am convinced that his subdued appearance was a part of his cunning plan. He allowed the women in the household to believe that they were in charge, and consequently they took care of all the responsibilities and made the important decisions and did most of the work, while he was able to take Janet Patricia to dancing classes and do all the other delightful things with his children that made life worth while. And if the women pressed him too hard to attend to something or go somewhere or see someone, he had an infallible loophole through which to escape: 'Yeah. I'll do it in a minute'. Thereafter, minutes could stretch to hours.

He handled his final sickness with the same quiet courage. He knew something was wrong but it was not in his nature to trouble others. As he grew thinner it became apparent that something serious was wrong, but even in face of the worst news he remained the same calm, quiet man he had always been. As time ran short he was happy to be able to visit his family in England and to maintain a clear and lucid mind right to the very end. His wife and family supported him throughout with the tender and thoughtful care that he deserved. They knew when to step in and when to step back, and carried him through it all as he would have wanted.

Those of us standing on the outside have no idea of the loss that Betty and her children have suffered. We can only offer our sympathy and pray that God will comfort them for the loss of a quietly wonderful husband and father, and that he will comfort all of us for the loss of a valued and respected parishioner.

Coda

The Teaching of Christ

Male chauvinist pigs and piglets – who talk disparagingly about women – are merely a pale reflection of the male chauvinist husbands and fathers who in days gone by ran their homes like army barracks and ordered their womenfolk around like slaves. Maybe they are still around, for it is not so long ago since I was the embarrassed witness of an example of such gross dictatorship. I was visiting a house and, while I was speaking to the husband, the wife came in and asked, very apologetically, 'Is it all right if I run over to Mary's for a few minutes?' He reacted like she had suggested selling their children into white slavery. Had she nothing better to do with her time, and hell she knew how to pick her moment to ask, and never fear, there would be more about this later – all the time giving me meaningful glances and waiting expectantly for an approving nod. The best I could do was to hold my ground until the poor woman had gone and then beat a silent and hasty retreat.

That man was convinced that he was right, because that is how he was brought up. He is merely one of the many misguided individuals who believe that if their conscience doesn't disturb them, they are all right. They firmly maintain that they will be safe before God if they feel no guilt about what they are doing. It's not just the wife-bullies who take this line, but every grade and shade of sinner from the petty thief to the murderer. 'I don't feel bad, therefore I've done no wrong'.

What standards are we applying to our behaviour, that we finish up with such strange results? Our intelligence? What we were taught at school? Tradition? The teaching of some philosopher or politician? The style and standards of the popular papers and TV programmes? Little wonder, then, that we feel no qualms of conscience. After all, not too many of them have ever bluntly said to us, 'Thou shalt not...'

Until we apply the teaching of Christ to our behaviour, and find no wrong in it, we cannot be sure of our acceptance into Heaven by God, the Father of Christ, and our Father.

Ordinary People

According to Butler's *Lives of the Saints*, St Philip Neri, from 'five years of age, was never known, in the least tittle, wilfully to transgress the will of his parents'.

It is enough to put you off saints for life! I am sure Philip was really nothing like this. He was probably a very normal, self-willed, rowdy little boy, but in Butler's day it was 'the done thing' to present saints as though they were paragons of virtue right from their earliest moments; or to quote a friend of mine, who had been asked to admire the angelic behaviour of a neighbour's children, 'They were a bunch of posy wee sickeners'.

The real saints were, first and foremost, real people. They had some virtues, and they had plenty of vices, but they struggled with their weaknesses and tried to show by their lives that they loved God and their neighbour. Modern writers, thankfully, have faced up to this fact, and they try to give us a true picture of the saints, 'warts and all'. Instead of starting out with predetermined notions of what a saint should be, they begin by looking at the saint's life and asking, 'What was it that made this very ordinary individual into an extraordinary saint?' The results are both fascinating and consoling, for the saints came from all walks of life, and, as today's lesson tells us, they all had a different set of gifts from God. St Thérèse never lost her childhood purity. St Augustine led a life of corruption and depravity in his youth. St John Vianney was a hopeless organiser. St Teresa of Avila was a most efficient and energetic manager. St Anthony of the Desert was as thin as a whip. St Thomas Aquinas was so fat that his friends cut a semi-circle in the table so that he could eat more comfortably. St Benedict Joseph Labre was a tramp and St Louis was a king.

The list is endless. They were all as different from one another as chalk and cheese, yet they were all united in their search for God. They took the strengths and the weaknesses that God had given them and within these limits they lived out their lives. We, instead, keep wishing and hoping for better gifts, consoling ourselves in the meantime for our failures by thinking of the good things we could do if only God had made us stronger or smarter or richer.

If God had wanted us to be different he would have made us different. For his own good reasons he made us as we are, and all he asks is that we use and develop the powers he has given us.

Free Will

A mad professor performed an experiment for his students. He set a flea on the table and then struck the table a mighty blow with his fist. The flea jumped two feet into the air. He then took a pair of scissors and cut off all the flea's legs, and again struck the table a mighty blow. The flea did not budge. 'From this', he said, 'we may conclude that the flea's sense of hearing is in its legs, since by removing its legs I have rendered the insect completely deaf!'

Believe it or not, most of us are guilty of this kind of crazy argument, not just once in a lifetime, but quite frequently. We argue that because event A occurs after event B, event A is occurring because of event B. You were caught in a shower of rain yesterday. Today you have a cold. Therefore, you conclude, the rain caused the cold. You saw a magpie on your way to work yesterday. Today you trip over a brush and break your leg. You have studied carefully all the conditions of the wind and tide before you cast your net. You catch a great haul of fish. Therefore, you conclude, the great haul is due to your expert knowledge.

Experience is the only effective deterrent to this kind of thinking. We have to learn, the hard way, that a lot of things happen no matter what great efforts we have made to promote them or what precautions we have taken to prevent them. With a snap of his fingers, God can turn the whole situation upside down. He can cause the most unlikely things to happen and he can prevent our most cherished efforts from producing results. 'By God's grace I am what I am', says St Paul, and it is by God's grace that we can do anything.

The really difficult question for us to understand and to answer is, 'Why then did God leave us free to do wrong things, to go against him?' It takes a great depth of generosity and understanding to love someone, and yet leave them free, to want their happiness so much that you even allow them to walk out of your life and never see them again. This is the kind of love God has for us. He does not tie us down, but he wishes with all his heart that we will come back to him.

Moving Towards God

As I was buying some trees in a garden centre, the nurseryman told me about visiting his vicar's garden recently, where there was a glorious display of plants and flowers. The vicar was rhapsodising on the beauty of God's creation and the bountifulness of the earth, but his gardener maintained a tight-lipped silence and looked on glumly. Eventually the vicar departed and the gardener turned to my nurseryman. 'It's all very well talking about the beauty of God's creation, but you should have seen this place before I came along'.

Unknowingly he had put his finger on a rather important theological point. God did indeed create the earth and all its beauty, but he gave it into our care, and if we fail to look after it and provide the right conditions for its growth, it will quickly lapse into chaos. The farmer cannot lie in his bed and hope that the fields will produce their crops automatically. He has to plough the ground and sow the seed and then he can wait while the Lord works the marvellous miracle of growth.

The Lord equally works marvels in the hearts of men, but he expects us to lay the groundwork by providing the right conditions for his Spirit to work its wonders. If any man turns away from evil, it is because the Spirit of God has moved his heart, but it is also because others, by their prayers and guidance and sacrifices, have encouraged him to open his heart to the Spirit. The first-time farmer ploughs his field because he has seen the crops that others have grown, and the evil man turns from his evil because he has seen the benefits that the God-fearing man enjoys.

Forgiveness

There is no machine quite as complicated as the human person.

In this age of science and technology, we are used to vast and intricate machines whose secrets only a few talented men can fathom, but the human body alone – taking no account at this point of the mind, the emotions and the soul – is a far more intricate and finely tuned machine than any that we have yet invented and one whose secrets no one has yet completely mastered.

Indeed, the great fascination of any form of biological research is the continuous revelation of layer upon layer of more delicate elements and patterns of life. No matter how closely we study the body, there always seems to be another and more intricate layer of life below the one we have just examined.

Add to all this the human mind, the emotions, the soul and all the possible interactions between them and you can see that the human person is a very complicated machine indeed. Any interference with one part will affect all the others, and, more notably, any danger to one part will damage the others.

Failure to forgive – ourselves and others – is a form of damage to the human person. It eats and gnaws at the human being like a cancer that devours all before it. There is no hiding place from its consequences. There is no protection from its germs. It influences all our decisions and actions, whether we admit it or not.

Forgive those who have trespassed against you. Failure to do so will harm you more than anything else. And then forgive yourself.

How Do You Kill God?

The real problems of the Apostle Thomas began, not when he denied the possibility of Christ having risen from the dead, but when he finally accepted the resurrection as a genuine and undeniable fact. For he was now left with a further and far more difficult question, 'How do you kill God?' If Christ the Son of God has risen from the dead, then who killed the Son of God?

The idea of the Son of God rising from the dead is not all that difficult to accept. After all we are talking about God – or the Son of God, which is really the same thing. If God has any meaning at all, it must emphasise his power over everything. If God is not in control, he is not God. So for God to rise from the dead is merely to say that God has control of life and death – or, to put it another way, he decides whether life will be present or absent. If God possesses this power over life, who can take it away from him? He can easily deal with any threats to himself by taking away the life of the threatener, so how can anyone take away God's life? It is like trying to kill a shadow. It lives on a different level altogether.

The answer is, no one. If Christ, the Son of God, had not made the decision to give up his own life for us, no one could have taken it from him. It is not only the suffering and death of Christ that redeemed us. The voluntary surrender of his place in Heaven as the Son of God; his right to authority over the entire world; his willingness to allow ordinary men and women to exercise power over him – all of these linked together made up the complete and supreme sacrifice of the Son of God for the human race.

The resurrection of Christ, the Son of God, with his power over life and death, is the easiest thing in the world to explain and to accept. It is the death of the Son of God that really defeats us.

Persecution

John the Baptist called on all men to turn away from their sins, and Herod reacted 'by shutting John up in prison'.

Jesus announced that he was the fulfilment of all the prophecies in scripture, and the Jews 'rose up and expelled him from the town, leading him to the brow of the hill on which it was built, intending to hurl him over the edge'.

St Peter and St John told the Jews that through their children 'all the families of the earth will be blessed', and 'they arrested them and put them in jail'.

St Paul preached that Jesus was the Son of God, and the Jews 'conspired to kill him', and even 'went so far as to keep close watch on the city gates day and night in an attempt to do away with him'.

St James preached that 'God has raised up Jesus to his right hand as ruler and saviour to bring repentance to Israel and forgiveness of sins', and Herod had him beheaded.

'If they persecuted me, they will persecute you too,' Jesus said. We need not be surprised if our efforts to turn to God and lead a good life are threatened. Only when we are making progress do the enemies of God feel the need to oppose us.

Doing the Right Thing

Every reasonable man takes pleasure in pointing out the faults of his neighbour. He experiences a certain sense of value and dependability when he highlights the worn-out principles and watery efforts of his rivals. He is not thereby displaying a particularly aggressive or vindictive turn of mind. He is merely recognising the weakness of his own defences, and taking consolation from the fact that his attackers may have a few problems of their own.

The non-practising Catholic has always found great consolation in this kind of behaviour, and when he finds a passage from scripture that seems to back him up he can hardly believe his luck. He immediately bombards everyone with scathing comments on the so-called Catholics – bowing and scraping, eating the altar rails, thumping their breasts and calling out, 'Lord, Lord', yet continuing to lead greedy, selfish and gossipy lives. Who would want to belong to a religion like that? Better to have nothing at all to do with them – which is exactly what he wanted from the start. Just a good enough excuse to drop the time- and energy-consuming practices that his parents and teachers had imposed on him in his youth. He does not have to believe in his excuse, as long as he is able to use it.

Let's face it. There are many bad Catholics. There is an even bigger number of poor Catholics, and there are very, very few good – much less perfect – Catholics. But one thing can be said for all of them. They *believe* in right and good behaviour, even though they may not always practise it. They are not always a great example, but at least they know it. The cynics who can quote the Scriptures and point smugly to the words of today's gospel, 'It is not those who say to me, 'Lord, Lord' who will enter the Kingdom of Heaven' have obviously forgotten that it was the terrified cry of Peter, 'Lord, save me', that brought Jesus to his rescue, and the humble prayer of the thief, 'Lord, remember me', that brought him salvation.

Calling 'Lord, Lord' may not get us into Heaven, but it stands a much better chance of bringing us near the gates than concocting spurious arguments in condemnation of others.

Trust in God

Men and women complain that God does not answer their prayers.

God complains that men and women do not listen to his answers.

We pray to be spared all pain and problems in life, in the belief that this is the true path to happiness.

God permits pain and problems because it is the only way most of us will learn about forgiveness, compassion and the things that lead to happiness.

Somewhere along the road of life, we have picked up the idea that God made a kind of deal with the human race. 'If you behave yourselves, I will be nice to you. If you sin, I will send misfortunes crashing down on you'.

It seems a reasonable bargain.

The only problem is that God never made any such agreement. Whatever the plan of God involves, it does not involve sparing 'good' people and punishing 'bad' people. Jesus had to run the gauntlet of suffering and he was supremely good. St Paul warns us, 'We all have to experience many hardships before we enter the Kingdom of God'.

It is important that we grasp this idea and hold on to it firmly because without it our faith will be blown away in times of crisis. When God pulls away the props, and we lose our family, our friends, our possessions and all the other things on which we leaned for happiness we find it very hard to trust, but that is what our faith is all about. 'If we suffer with him, we shall also reign with him'.

Man Plans and God Laughs

According to a supplement I was reading yesterday, a most unlikely book has become a contender for the Christmas best-seller list. It's *The Voices of Morebath* by Professor Eamon Duffy and it recounts the history of a tiny parish in a remote part of Devon between the years 1520 and 1574. Not the kind of project that has publishers reaching for their cheque books, but for some obscure reason it has caught the attention of a widespread of occasional readers as well as the expected clergy and historians.

For myself, the book's fascination lies in the detailed picture of parish life that the author conjures from the records kept by the parish priest, Sir Christopher Trychay (in those days a parish priest was called Sir instead of Father), and the inevitable comparison with parish life today. The similarities are startling, indeed a bit frightening. The same focus on running repairs to the parish buildings, hiring of plumbers and joiners, bricklayers and roofers, attending meetings, keeping accounts, settling disputes and, of course, raising money. They had a marvellous system for raising money. Each family had to keep a number of sheep for the parish, depending on their wealth. They fed these sheep over the winter and when spring came the wool was sold off on behalf of the parish.

The system worked very well, but the Reformation was on the way and the parish was about to be taken apart at the seams. For example, Sir Christopher had brought a statue of St Sidwell to Morebath with him and for twenty years had tirelessly promoted devotions to her , and now statues were declared unlawful. He had coaxed and persuaded his parishioners for twenty-nine years to support his fund for buying a set of black vestments for requiem Masses, but only a fortnight after the vestments were bought,

Masses for the dead were outlawed. The parish sheep were sold off, the church hall was rented out, parish entertainments were forbidden, candles, banners, vestments, statues, paintings, even sacred vessels were sold off. In one year, a life's work was demolished, but somehow Sir Christopher survived – for another twenty-five years. Like the rest of us, he discovered the hard way that if you want to make God laugh, you tell him about your plans for the future.

Looking Ahead to the Millennium

The forthcoming millennium is, in my opinion, a once-in-a-lifetime business opportunity, and nothing more. Experience has taught me that behind every celebration, of whatever noble cause or event, even though it is given respectful and suitable mention in all branches of the media, there is a little man with a briefcase in a back room somewhere controlling every facet of the occasion and skimming ten per cent off the top.

The only solid contribution to the millennium debate that I have heard so far has been made by Spike Milligan, who, when asked what he intended doing for the millennium, said that he was 'going to bed'. I intend to follow his example. I detest Hogmanay parties. In fact I detest nearly all parties that will not fit into a small room. I usually turn the TV off on New Year's Eve and see in the new year to the troubled strains of César Franck's Symphony in D Minor. It beats any party.

The theory that the millennium really began on the first day of 1999 is complicated by the fact that most authorities would now agree that Christ was born several years before what is now known as the Christian era. Moreover, there would be no millennium at all if we had adopted a binary system of mathematics – or indeed any other system – rather than the decimal one that has been handed down to us. So we are merely celebrating the approximate lapse of two thousand years since the birth of Christ, rather than an exact and definite figure.

This will matter little to most Christians – or indeed to most people – since, as the Bible tells us, 'A thousand years are like yesterday come and gone, no more than a watch in the night'. Alongside the hundreds of millions of years since the world began, our life on this planet is the blink of an eye, and alongside the years of eternity – if we can put it that way – it has no duration at all.

Reasonable though it may be to celebrate this occasion, if we are expecting the beginning of a new age, or even the disappearance of some of the worst elements of the old age, we are in for a disappointment. How many new years have we celebrated in the past with ardent wishes for a Happy New Year, only to find that it was as sinful and as selfish and as ruthless as the year we had left behind. For that reason, the approach of the millennium clearly demands an honest and stringent assessment by all the Christian Churches of their performance to date.

We have to ask ourselves, 'What progress have we made in the past two thousand years?' Are we making steady advances or are we on an everlasting roller coaster, reaching the hearts of people today and being dismissed as irrelevant, or even worse, tomorrow? Certainly, the Catholic Church has taken a terrible tumble in the past twenty years. From the heights of euphoria as the pope visited Ireland in 1979, we have begun a rugged and bone-shaking descent, past Bishop Casey and Fr Brendan Smith, and the institutions of Church and state where child abuse was endemic, down to the flatlands of reality where we desperately try to regain some of our self-esteem by protesting to the world that the present perception of the priesthood as inevitably linked with abuse is a total and callous lie, and that we merely take our place among the sinners of this world, sadly no better, but certainly no worse than any of our Christian colleagues.

Today, the Church stands behind the starting line, handicapped by the weight of its recent sins and struggling to make a decent showing in the race of life. It still tends to equate power with influence – instead of listening to the wisdom that the Spirit assures us is found in the people of God, it issues more rules and regulations and sparingly doles out the powers and permissions that are its patrimony, lest we think we had a right to any of them.

I must admit, even I have been amazed by the central miserliness of the Roman bureaucrats, who think the year 2000 is not really important enough to merit the use of a general absolution formula for the ordinary members of the Church, but permits it on a permanent basis to members of the armed forces of the world whose regular occupation is killing people. It would be nice if they could move from some of their entrenched positions without waiting to be blown out of them by the people of God.

As the years catch up with us we hope that the rapidly accelerating rate of medical and technological development will create a world in which life itself would be prolonged and the quality of life enhanced, but instead it has led to a world in which economic factors determine how we shall – or shall not – share in the medical advances that have the power to preserve our lives, and where political advantage – and note that I am not saying political necessity – is more likely than ever to determine whether we shall live or die.

This century has seen the most savage and widespread wars of all time, and the killing of more combatants than all the wars put together that have been waged since the beginning of time. Prophets of peace and the New Jerusalem have come and gone, some leaving a legacy of unequalled violence and barbarity.

We have witnessed in this century the death of so many civilians that even now we are unable to give an accurate estimate of how many have perished. Their only crime was to be born into this ghastly century, who were in the wrong place at the wrong time and, as a consequence, died a brutal death.

Christ told us to love one another as he has loved us; to lay down our lives for one another as he laid down his life for us; to share with one another as he has shared everything with us; to be friends to one another as he was a friend to us; to forgive one another as he has forgiven all of us; to be one as he and the Father are one.

We might ask if there is anything good to remember, and it has to be said that some people have moved out of their isolation and have gratefully adopted the wisdom to be found in all the other faiths and religions, and have rejoiced in the community that we share with every living human being on our journey towards an eternal Kingdom. Some have volunteered their lives and their energies to the care of the persecuted and the afflicted, wherever they are to be found.

We enjoy better health, better living standards, better education than those who have gone before us but, sadly, we have no urge to make sure that everyone else enjoys those benefits also

In the path of progress, the millennium is really a distraction. There will be little work of any kind done until it has passed. Undoubtedly, the spirit of God will still be with us as we move into this new era and it may blow us in directions that we have never anticipated.

If we can be persuaded to listen to the spirit, to hear what it is saying to the churches, then maybe we will find a new power and a new determination to restore all things in Christ.

Already, the symptoms of millennium overload are beginning to show. The 'parties to end all parties' are being cancelled for lack of interest. The publicans are talking of closing up shop for the duration because they cannot afford the wages being demanded by their staff, unless they put another pound on the price of beer, and that is hardly likely to endear them to the punters.

I think it is safe to say that a record amount of alcohol will be consumed over the holidays, and it will take a lot longer than usual to get people back to their normal working patterns, but rather than finding themselves on the threshold of a new age, hungry for the chance of pursuing new goals and exploiting new opportunities, most people will, I suspect, find the new millennium merely another – but vastly more horrendous – morning after the night before.

Remembrance

Remembrance is a universal tradition, but a personal instinct. Every remembrance is individual. For some it is a vivid moment from their own experience. For me it is the memory as an eight-year-old of leaning over a gate on my way home from school to watch the soldiers from the local depot undergoing training in the ways of war. They fought make-believe battles against make-believe enemies and took winning so seriously that they lay in long-suffering silence among the nettles and thistles of County Tyrone without a whisper of complaint. But, inevitably, we children sabotaged their plans and revealed their positions, leaving them to trudge home, stung by nettles, pricked by thistles, wet, tired, grimy and disillusioned, but that is the nature of soldiering.

For the young and the not-so-young, remembrance is the response to what an older generation has passed on to them or to what they have seen on TV or read in the papers; and for all, it is the silent awareness that those who have gone to war have left a part, if not all, of themselves behind on the battlefield. Even those who survived have died a little.

And where is the all-powerful God, our loving Father, in the midst of this chaos? Like many another parent, he is calling in vain to his children, 'Do not fight, do not kill. Learn to love one another'. If we do not remember the past, we are doomed to repeat it.

Love Your Enemies

The sheer emotional power of Remembrance Day ceremonies can be too much for those who have survived the terrors of real warfare. Tears overflow onto wrinkled cheeks and hands begin to tremble as they try to hold the awful pain of what they have endured at a safe distance – but it will not be denied. The tears return, and even at a distance of sixty years the memories of death and danger set the ageing body trembling once again.

War is such an awful activity. It doesn't ask, 'Do you want to join?' It drags us into a conflict that we had no hand in starting and allows us no say in how it might be resolved. It demands obedience to reckless orders and subordinates us to a false culture where the only important thing is winning. And it doesn't work that way. War does not end war. It merely provides the pretext for the next war. I am not suggesting that we do not have to defend ourselves, but it is more important to understand the enemy than to defeat him. If we do not understand him, we are doomed to eternal warfare with him. If we cannot accept the diversity of life and culture that surrounds us, we will spend our lives trying to compel people to agree with us, and we will look with suspicion on anything that is not familiar to us.

Lyndon B. Johnson was told that the people of Thailand did not go in for handshaking or any other kind of physical contact. And how did he use this information? He told the world that if handshaking was good enough for the people of God's own country it should be good enough for Thailand, and for good measure he gave everyone he met there a double handshake.

I get very nervous when I hear presidents or prime ministers talking about war, especially war against terrorism, for terrorism is not a person. It is an idea, a method, a technique, and you cannot go to war with a technique. You go to war with a person, and if it is the wrong person you have not merely failed, you have started another war. But even if you attack the right person and defeat him you still haven't understood him. And understanding is your only hope for the future. Christ summed it all up very effectively. He said, 'Love your enemies'.

Interests

Leaving aside what I might call my professional work on the grounds that you already know enough about it, I just want to say a few words about three activities that have interested me a great deal throughout my life. First was writing, second was music and third was photography, though not necessarily in that order.

I took an interest in writing in my grammar school days, but a teacher once told me that I could not write English and that scuppered my interest in writing. That was how it was in those days. There was no suggestion that you might have a certain talent. It was assumed that if you had any talent it would show through eventually, with or without encouragement. I had to wait until my mid-forties before someone suggested that I might have some writing ability, and that saw the beginning of my writing career, such as it was. Believe it or not I began writing for radio. I had done countless broadcasts – for BBC Radio Foyle, Radio Ulster, Radio 4 and the World Service – before I had anything published. In fact, I had done more than a hundred thoughts for the day before I decided to publish them myself in book form, and they were very well received.

Very few pieces that I have written were intended for publication. They were nearly all intended for broadcasting or for delivery at some function, with just a few exceptions, and that set the tone for them. They could not afford to be dull. If you were dull you lost your audience with the flick of a switch, and being lively and interesting all the time was never easy. Even such a serious subject as Good Friday had to be fresh and different if people were going to even look into the book. My most recent book, *Life, Death and the Bits in Between*, had to have a light-hearted theme running through it if it was to capture the attention of the general public, not to mention the need for every book to have a strong promotional team who would push the book and extol its virtues at every opportunity.

My second interest is music. I loved to listen to classical music even from my earliest days, but there was always an attitude of criticism or disbelief among one's contemporaries. They found it hard to believe that you might enjoy a more complex form of music than they were used to hearing on Radio Luxembourg. Personally I found no difficulty bridging the gap, and when I was well into my pastoral work experience I was able to encourage, if not help in some way, some of the young people in my parish who had found a new interest in singing. One young lady, in particular, impressed me with her talents, and for the next twenty years I did what I could to help her with her career. If you want to hear her sing, just tap YouTube and the name Gemma Hasson into your computer and take your choice.

My third interest is photography and this was an obsession from my student days. Sadly, it has all changed since then. In those days you set out with your 35-mm camera, or maybe with something a little less exotic, but you could freely photograph whatever took your attention and the only criterion was: 'Is this a Good Photograph?' Today it is almost a hanging offence to take photographs in public without written permission.

In addition to the hazards of wielding a camera in public nowadays, no one warned us about the hazards of transferring our precious analogue negatives to the computer hard drive. Briefly, if you do not know what you are doing you can reduce the quality of your precious archive photos from the limitless potential of even a 35-mm negative to the pixelated fuzziness of a primitive telephone camera.

I was able to get most of my negatives of the Traveller family published before they were either lost or ruined, but I shudder to think how many negatives I have thrown out over the years, how much history I have dumped into the bins in recent years only to realise that there is nothing from the past that does not become a treasure of antiquity with every passing year.

The Thin End of the Wedge

Have you ever figured why it is so much easier to drive a nail that has a point to it than one that is blunt? Or why it is that even a small wedge can split quite a big piece of timber?

When we talk about 'the thin end of the wedge', we are issuing a warning. Something undesirable will happen unless we take great care. And if it happens, it will draw a thousand other undesirable events behind it. It is the perfect picture of temptation. If I offer to make you president of the US if you shoot your grandmother, you will have no trouble dealing with the temptation – unless your granny has been giving you a particularly hard time – but if I offer to make you president of the football club if you will skip visiting your grandmother on Sunday afternoons, you may find the temptation a lot harder to deal with.

Given enough time, we are capable of any atrocity. To begin with, we may recoil from uttering even a harsh word. To finish, we can blow someone's brains out and tell ourselves that it is right and good. Temptation makes no frontal attack. It sneaks up on us and nibbles away at our defences – like woodworm. Then, when a serious storm breaks over us, we crumble under the attack.

The Feast of the Baptism of the Lord

The Baptism of Christ was completely unnecessary – except as an example and an encouragement. He was founding a new family through which everyone would find their way to Heaven, and the acceptance or initiation ceremony was to be Baptism. It made no sense to ask the founding father of the family to go through the joining-up ceremony; but that is precisely what he did – in order to encourage and to convince us.

At Baptism we are adopted into a new family. We are 'born again', in the words of Christ, into this group of people whose one, unifying principle is the Spirit of God, which they, in turn, received at Baptism. Christ alone did not need Baptism, for he has always possessed the Spirit of God, but when he came on earth he invited his apostles to share that spirit, and they in turn have invited succeeding generations into this new 'family'. If God were to pull aside the veil at the Baptism of your child to show you the Spirit descending from Heaven and taking up his abode in the heart of this tiny baby as he did with the apostles – including flames of fire and everything else – how proud you would be that your child is now the home of God's Spirit on earth. Unfortunately, we approach the admission of our child into God's Church with less excitement than we do admission into a football club, leaving most of the follow-up in the hands of fate or chance or a willing granny.

We would never dream of such thoughtlessness on a physical level. From the moment of birth our baby is cuddled and comforted and given the ultimate in care and attention because we want that delicate little body to grow into a strong, healthy, secure adult, not a nervous crackpot. At a spiritual level we can be guilty of the most glaring neglect. We baptise a child, give it a new kind of life – the life of God himself – and then leave that life to wither away and die from neglect.

The life of God comes in delicate form at Baptism – just as human life in a baby is still delicate. If it is not nourished and protected it will die, from exposure to sin and bad example and corruption, just as its human life will die from exposure to cold and hunger and neglect.

Baptism is the starting point of God's life in us, not the finishing point. We begin our spiritual lives as Catholics. We want to be able to finish them as good Catholics.

The Book of Job

The Book of Job has a serious problem. It has a happy ending. Remember, if you can, back in the 1950s, Hollywood used to produce what it called biblical epics, but they were what the man in the back row of the cinema tended to call 'sex and sand movies', and they were forever being called to account because they distorted the text of the Bible and blithely introduced a romantic interest or a happy ending where none existed.

Now, had they looked at the Book of Job they would have realised that here was the first genuine, romantic Hollywood film script, ready for use – rich parents, good-looking, successful and happy children. Then tragedy hits – death of children, loss of possessions, sickness, loneliness and despair; but our hero never gives up. He never doubts God's goodness, and in the final reel, he is rewarded for his fidelity. All the friends and possessions that anyone could ask for are restored to him. His health recovers. His wife learns to love him again. His children grow healthy and strong. He is the ultimate hero – the winner that every movie-goer wants to be.

Sadly, life is rarely quite so romantic. In the real battle of everyday life, when misfortune and sickness come to visit us, they often come to stay. Job himself was ready to believe that his time had come. In fact, there were times when he hoped that death would come, for his sickness was so overpowering and his spirit was so low that death would have been a welcome release. But he also clung to the belief that God was a just God, and because he had not sinned God would restore him to his former glory.

In Job's day the diagnosis of illness was primitive, to say the least. People knew that they were sick, that they felt awful, but they had no way of knowing whether the violent sickness they were experiencing was an indicator of serious internal problems or merely the inevitable consequence of trying to set a new beer drinking record the night before. But there was always the consolation that the ailment, however vicious, might only be temporary and that come next Tuesday you would be back on your feet, ready to take up life where you left off. And that was why Job never lost hope. There was always the possibility of healing, and in his case it turned out to be true.

All of which is scant consolation to the man or woman of our day who has been told that the tumour is malignant or the cancer has invaded the liver or the leukaemia has defeated all attempts at treatment. Modern medicine has the power to diagnose our ailments more quickly and accurately, but it also has the power to tell us that – short of a miracle – our days are numbered and nothing can be done to extend them. What consolation, then, do we offer these people?

Or if the years have taken their toll and we can no longer move of our own accord or take care of our most fundamental needs, who is going to console us? Or rather, how can they console us when we know that each year, indeed each day, leaves us less active, less mobile, less independent, and that ultimately the only escape is death? A few years ago a friend of mine suffered a stroke and for four and a half years she lay in hospitals and nursing homes unable to move any part of her body except her left arm. But she could hear and speak, so it was possible to interest her in the people she knew, in the comings and goings of her neighbours, and even to invent a few dramatic incidents to spice up the staid routine of her former life. But I have also known a woman who for twelve years lay completely immobile, unable to move, unable to speak, yet clearly in touch with this world and with all around her. What does the Book of Job have to say to her?

Not a great deal, if our purpose is to escape the pain and the isolation and the dependence, but a great deal if our purpose is to confront them. Job's friends wanted him to complain, then accuse God or somebody of giving him a raw deal. He could then tell everyone who came along about the injustice God had done to him, how badly he had been treated. Instead he embraced his sufferings – 'The Lord has given. The Lord has taken away; blessed be the name of the Lord'. We cannot avoid being affected emotionally or even weeping a little as we confront sickness or infirmity or death. The cynic will say, 'I thought Heaven was supposed to be such a wonderful place – why are you so slow to get there?' What he doesn't know is that there are holy men and women in every generation who have come to know God so intimately – or rather those to whom God has revealed himself so intimately – that they experience a burning desire to leave this world and be united for ever with God. St Paul was a perfect example. But the rest of us, we are not perfect Christians. We are designed and built by God to protect our lives above everything else, so when the moment comes for us to let go of it we find ourselves struggling. Even so, I have seen people embrace their sickness and approaching death with devastating effect. Their fear of death, if we may call it that, was more the fear of separation than the fear of God or of punishment. They wept, as an exile might have wept before the emigrant ship, but there were no outbursts. (In fact, the only man who did not weep frightened me a little with his calmness. I would have felt more at home with a few tears.)

Our contribution to life is not determined by strength of body or sharpness of mind or length of years. Like the widow's mite it is determined by sincerity. We give what we can, and if God has confined us to a chair in the corner where we watch life hustle by then that is what we give. It is not a negative gift. It is a powerfully positive and effective gift that flows from our very presence, from our merely being there, rather than doing anything. And the more care and affection and time our family and friends devote to us the greater their sense of loss when we finally go. The parent or grandparent who lay motionless and silent for years leaves a great gap in our lives, a dark hole, that we vainly try to understand. The sick and the infirm wield a powerful influence upon our lives. Sometimes they give us a reason to live. Sometimes they prove the futility of just doing things, sometimes they open our hearts to a hitherto unknown world of patience, of sacrifice, and of love in its deepest form – the love of God that is still, silent and infinite.

Marian Devotion in Irish Tradition

Let me begin this talk where it should end. On 29 October 1963 the Second Vatican Council decided, by a majority of two per cent, to treat the discussion on Mary as part of the Document on the Church and not as a separate document, a fairly massive break from the traditional thinking of the time. They emphasised that they did not intend to underrate Our Lady's place in the Church in any way, but the impression was given to the outside world that there was disagreement among the council bishops, and it was not entirely unwarranted. When it came to the text itself there was a great deal of debate, but the fairly brisk way in which the council fathers dealt with the various questions came as a big disappointment to the traditional supporters of Marian devotion.

Firstly, they said they did not wish to decide those questions about Our Lady which had not been fully explained and clarified by theologians. While acknowledging – and they could hardly do otherwise – that our Lady was 'blessed', both according to the Scriptures – 'from this day forward all generations will call me blessed' – and because she was the one who 'heard the word of God and kept it', they balked at the idea of addressing her as 'Mediator of all graces'. They quoted St Paul: 'One God and one mediator between God and man Christ Jesus', and pointed out that Our Lady's influence flows from the merits of Christ; they finally acknowledged that the Church has invoked Mary under the titles of Advocate, Helper, Benefactress and Mediator but they immediately added, 'This, however, is so understood that it neither takes away anything from nor adds anything to the dignity and efficacy of Christ the one mediator'. And the next paragraph begins: 'The Church does not hesitate to profess this subordinate role of Mary which it constantly experiences and recommends to the heartfelt attention of the faithful'.

It is clear, then, that the Council had no intention of immersing itself in the controversies surrounding Marian devotion and Marian titles. So when you next quote the pope, any pope, in support of your favourite novena or pilgrimage or even, God forbid, moving statue, remember that the official voice of the Church, speaking through the Vatican Council, is very wary of giving new titles and new roles to Our Lady.

With that in mind, let's go back to the beginning of Irish devotion to Mary. And here we find a happy coincidence that links this city of Derry to some of the earliest written references to Marian devotion in Ireland, at the time of St Patrick. In 431, the Council of Ephesus declared Mary to be the Mother of God, and the word was bound to have reached Ireland by the time St Patrick arrived here. It could indeed be true, but we are talking about the first written reference to Marian devotion, and it has a very distinct and definite connection to the city of Derry.

Most of you probably know the name Adamnan – or as we call him today, Eunan – the writer of the life of St Columba. He was one of Columba's successors as abbot of Iona about a hundred years after Columba's death, and he wrote both the life of Columba and another book called *De Locis Sanctis* (Concerning the Holy Places), and in it he talks about a church that he has heard about in Palestine, dedicated to 'Blessed Mary Ever Virgin'. A short time later we have another document called Adamnan's Law, published at a Synod in Birr, County Offaly, in 697, which sought to improve the condition of women by exempting them from military service. 'It would be as sinful', it argues, 'to kill in battle the mother of a child as it would be to kill in battle Mary the Mother of Jesus'. And in the year 700, the poet Cucuimne wrote a long poem in Latin in honour of Our Lady; the experts conclude that Iona, Columba's monastery, was its place of origin. So we find from the very earliest times a connection between Derry and devotion to Mary, the Mother of God.

In fact, from the seventh to the seventeenth century, there is a steadily increasing output of poems and litanies and hymns from the Irish bards and the scribes; many are poems describing events in people's lives involving Our Lady. Others are addressed to Our Lady, invoking her help under various titles that have been heaped upon her over the years, and some are descriptive of Mary's pain and sacrifice. In the fifteenth century, Tuathail Ó Huiginn wrote of her: 'On Friday Mary stayed by him; though she bore much of what he bore, she saw no dishonour in her son being taken from her. What more terrible for Mary than to watch his pain, yet she stays by him; sorrow like hers I know not of'. And in a tract from the same century Christ speaks to people about his sufferings and Mary's part in them. 'For she could not speak a word as she was standing under the Cross and her heart was as though broken. It was no wonder her suffering was so great because of the pain of death that I was suffering. That is why I said 'Eli Eli lama sabachtani''.

In the middle ages and later, we find evidence of devotion to Mary in an organised fashion in the many guilds dedicated to her. A guild was an organisation formed by bringing together the members of a particular profession – tailors, for example – which enabled them to set standard prices, settle wage disputes, buy materials in bulk and generally protect their interests. The tailors paid into a central fund, which was used to hire a chaplain who recited the Divine Office every day and offered Mass for the guild on specific occasions, in their headquarters in Fishamble Street in Dublin.

By the twelfth century, the Rosary had become a widespread form of devotion, and in the middle of the fifteenth century a lady called Iathvhreac mourns the death of her husband in a very moving poem as she looks at his rosary beads.

> I grieve for the death of him whose hand
> you did entwine each hour of prayer;
> my grief that is lifeless now
> and I no longer see it there.
> May Mary Mother, the king's nurse
> guard each path I follow here
> and may her son watch over me,
> O Rosary that recalled my tear.

From the twelfth to the sixteenth century, there were numerous forms of devotion to Mary, numerous prayers and poems written in her honour, and devotion to Mary had been integrated into quite a lot of the liturgies and ceremonies that would have been commonplace at that time. It is interesting to note that at the installation ceremony of the Lord Deputy in Dublin on Whit Sunday 1556, the outgoing deputy, Sir Anthony St Ledger, rode from Kilmainham to Christ Church and went straight to the Lady Chapel, where he knelt and heard Mass devoutly while the incoming Lord Deputy knelt a little distance away. After Mass, the patent of the new Lord Deputy was read aloud while the outgoing deputy knelt before the altar, and when the reading was finished the outgoing deputy yielded his place to his successor, and on his knees before the altar and at Our Lady's feet, he surrendered his sword of state to the new Lord Deputy; but this was probably the last occasion on which that ceremony was carried out.

The Reformation and the Penal Laws inevitably meant that public devotion to Our Lady was greatly curtailed, but there is much evidence that poems in honour of Our Lady and hymns and prayers and sermons about Our Lady continued to be written and preached wherever possible. The recitation of the Rosary became a substitute for the liturgies of the Eucharist which were forbidden to the Catholic community, and it was at about this time that the recital of the Rosary as a family prayer began to achieve some popularity.

In the nineteenth century, however, the laws against Catholics were greatly relaxed and, as a consequence, many of the devotions that were popular on the continent began to find their place among the Catholics of Ireland. In 1814, we find a priest in Dublin introducing the devotion of the first Saturday of each month in honour of the Immaculate Heart of Mary, a devotion that had been popular in France during the preceding century. In 1818, we find the Ursuline Sisters in Waterford introducing May Devotions for the first time. Devotion to the Brown Scapular, which was worn in honour of Our Lady of Mount Carmel, became very popular in the early part of the century and has continued right down to the present day. We also find a prayerbook called the Little Office of the Immaculate Conception being used among ordinary people at the beginning of the century, and it is still being used more than a hundred years later. In their early years, the Christian Brothers introduced a timetable in their schools where the Hail Mary was said when the clock struck each hour, and at the end of the day they recited the Litany of Our Lady and the Hail Holy Queen, a practice that survived to my own schooldays.

Perhaps most intriguing of all is the practice of prayer and devotion to Our Lady by public figures such as Daniel O'Connell. O'Connell was a very pious man. Even when he was travelling around on his political business, he observed the full Lenten fast, which in those days was quite strict – in fact, his wife feared that he would undermine his health – and he could be seen in the precincts of the Houses of Parliament saying his Rosary. The Rosary was said every night in his home, and when the Angelus bell rang it did not matter even if he was pursuing a fox on the hunting field – he stopped to recite the Angelus.

The apparitions at Knock in County Mayo on 21 August 1879 gave rise to great popular devotion to Our Lady. The authenticity and genuineness of the apparitions has been questioned with each generation, but if one applies the maxim that 'by their fruits you shall know them', then we cannot deny that something extraordinary happened on that date. Popular devotion to Mary in Ireland is not a complicated or deeply theological practice. It is based on the very simple belief that Mary, being the mother of Jesus, the Son of God, has more influence with her son than any of us, so we should enlist her help when we want to receive a favour from God. It is effectively summed up in this prayer-poem which was popular in nineteenth-century Ireland.

Blessed Mary be merciful to me
speak to God on my behalf,
tell him that I am but a poor creature
full of sins from head to toe
but I love you dear mother.
My love,
plead for me with Heaven's creator
and I will be ever grateful to you.

When we come to the twentieth century, it is ironic that one of the landmark incidents of its early years, the sinking of the *Titanic*, should also be an occasion where the devotion of Irish people to the Rosary was observed and noted by the entire world. A reporter interviewed a girl called Margaret Devaney, who was one of the forty Irish girls who were saved from the *Titanic*. He asked her what she did as the *Titanic* was sinking, and she replied, with tears in her eyes, 'I said my Rosary'. 'For yourself?', he asked, and she replied, 'Oh no, I never even thought of myself. For those whose drowning cries I heard in the water'.

In the same way the Rosary was recited in all the critical situations of life that occurred in the early part of the twentieth century, especially the First World War. During the Easter Rising, Joseph O'Connor, who was part of the garrison in Boland's Mills recorded: 'On Wednesday night, I was able to relieve one section that moved into a railway shed for food and sleep. After a while I looked in to see if they were sleeping well and my surprise was great when I found them all reciting the Rosary, the Section Commander giving out the prayers and the others responding'. And even the men in the General Post Office recalled that 'the Rosary was recited by some of us in turn almost every half hour of the four days and four nights we were on the roof'. When the mother of Patrick Pearse asked him to compose some prayer or poem for her to remember him by he gave her this little prayer.

> Dear Mary, thou didst see thy first-born son
> go forth to die amidst the scorn of men
> for whom he died,
> receive my first-born son into thy arms,
> who also hath gone out to die for men,
> and keep him by thee till I come to him;
> dear Mary I have shared thy sorrow,
> and soon shall share thy joy.

Devotion to Mary continued into and past the middle of the twentieth century. Even Brendan Behan made his contribution.

In that time of affliction, O Mother Mary
with no respite and my soul alone
but the saving grasp of your hand in my hand
in that trembling voyage to the heavenly throne …
don't ever abandon me, Mother Mary,
without your grace as a shield to wear …
when I'm run to earth and my lungs panting,
at the hunt's end and death in my face;
trembling, red-eyed while the hounds are baying;
O Mother, don't ever deny your grace.

In his dealings with us, God works all the time in a sacramental fashion. In other words, he acts through material, tangible things and physical, visible people, to communicate with us and to help us, because we do not understand anything else. We learn through seeing, speaking, listening, questioning, and relating in other ways to other human beings. This is how God relates to us – through other human beings. He became man through the Virgin Mary. He formed his Church through the apostles. He spread his Church over the world and down the ages through new apostles who as bishops or priests or lay people spread the good news all over the world that we are saved through Christ. If he uses all of us to do this work why would he not use Our Lady? She is the most perfect and willing follower that he has and as a woman she speaks loudly and clearly to one half of the human race in a way in which others cannot. She is the highest glory of the human race. Alongside her the apostles and the saints are mere imitations.

Forms of devotion to her will reflect the culture of our day and of our land. What was appropriate a hundred years ago may have no message or meaning for today's Christian. If that is true, then we must let go of these old forms of devotion and find new and relevant forms of prayer that speak to an age dominated by the computer and the TV and the internet.

As for the apparitions, the revelations and the happenings of our own day? Whether we like it or not, neither Lourdes nor Fatima nor Medjugorje nor Knock nor Melleray nor any other place of pilgrimage forms any part of the basic faith of Catholics.

If you so wish you do not need to believe in these apparitions or revelations. They have no binding force on anyone except perhaps on those who experience them. If you find solace in these events, then be thankful to God, but do not ever imagine that what was beneficial to your faith is essential to the faith of others.

It might, however, be useful to ask, 'When the next war comes to Ireland, and it inevitably will, as long as war exists, and the bombs are falling around our descendants as they huddle in the darkness, what prayer will they recite together to their God for grace and salvation?' Our ancestors endured persecution and degradation for maintaining their Catholic faith. And when the consolation of the Mass and the sacraments was taken from them they prayed the Rosary together, their personal profession of faith. Their devotion to Mary was summed up in this rhyming version of the 'Hail Holy Queen' – easier to remember in this way:

Hail, Holy Queen of mercy, parent hail,
Life, hope and comfort of this earthly vale
To thee we banished children loudly cry
With sighs and tears we supplicant do fly
Thrice glorious advocate exert thy love
And let those vows thine eyes of pity move
This exile past, o clement maid, obtain
That we may Jesus see and with him reign.

Devotion to Mary in Ireland hinges round our sinful nature and our failure to control it, but there is a pity, a compassion to it that says, 'No matter how far you have strayed, you are still Mary's child and she will protect you'. Past generations have spoken to her in the prayers they knew by heart from their infancy, but what prayer will coming generations recite? What faith will they defend to the death?